VESTED INTEREST

Also by Stephan Lesher

A CORONARY EVENT, with Michael Halberstam, M.D.

VESTED INTEREST

by
CHARLES B. LIPSEN

with
STEPHAN LESHER

DOUBLEDAY & COMPANY, INC. • GARDEN CITY, NEW YORK
1977

Library of Congress Cataloging in Publication Data

Lipsen, Charles B
Vested interest.

1. Lobbying—United States.   2. Lobbyists—
United States—Biography.   I. Lesher, Stephan,
joint author.   II. Title.
JK1118.L56   328.73′07′8
ISBN: 0-385-11470-2
Library of Congress Catalog Card Number 76–18359

For the women in our lives who, in their own ways, have suffered with us and supported us: Janice, Linda, and Sydney Lipsen; Sandi Lee; and Nancy Ball.

Introduction

In collaborating on *Vested Interest*, I considered several obvious but crucial questions:

—Why Chuck Lipsen? What qualified him as representative of the thousands of lobbyists in Washington?

—And would he be candid enough to make the book more than a soporific defense of a business long in question in America?

My early meetings with Lipsen assuaged my doubts.

For one thing, this was not to be a book about lobbies and lobbying in general. It was to be a book about a man who happens to be a lobbyist—who he is, what he does and how he does it. Lipsen was the ideal representative because he was neither the super-lobbyist whose peculiar expertise or fleeting high-powered connections placed him in the six-figure bracket of income like a handful in Washington, nor was he among that klatch of gray-flannel con men who squeeze out a living by taking advantage of the gullibility and ignorance of Washington politics that so often characterize people with a problem who live in Dubuque or Pasadena. Rather, he typified the thousands of hard-working lobbyists who, more often than not, deal honestly with their clients and the Congress if not always with the public. Besides, many of my friends in Congress had told me of his effectiveness in his work.

At least as important, Lipsen quickly looked on me as his counselor, someone in whom he could confide nearly everything concerning his thoughts and actions regarding an issue and be assured of my understanding and my pledge to treat his life and his work with sensitivity.

The result is an extraordinarily honest account which does not so much defend lobbying as explain it, does not excuse actions of congressmen or lobbyists but instead recounts them in context, does not so much laud lobbying as a constitutional right but supports it as a practical, democratic necessity.

Last, but hardly least, Lipsen's remarkable memory for detail, his wit and ability to laugh at his own foibles make this book precisely what we intended—a human story filled with insight into the lobbyist himself and the people with whom his life entwined personally and professionally.

In telling his story, Lipsen can lay claim to placing lobbying—honest, straightforward lobbying—on a plane with government itself; nobody trusts it but nearly everybody depends on it in a crisis.

STEPHAN LESHER

Washington, D.C.

1

MY SON,
THE LOBBYIST

In late 1975, then-President Ford walked into the Sheraton
Carlton Hotel in Washington as the main attraction of a $100-a-
ticket fund-raising party to help finance the re-election of Representative John Rhodes of Arizona, the Republican leader in the
House of Representatives.

I made sure I was among the first to grab the President's hand
while the flashbulbs were still popping and the TV cameras were
rolling.

"Hi, Mr. President," I said. "I'm Chuck Lipsen. I'm a Democrat"—he smiled—"but I'm also a lobbyist." His smile broadened.
He knew that while I was from The Other Political Faith, I was
also among that legion of Washingtonians—about 2,500 of us at
any given time—who put their money where their professional,
rather than political, interests lay.

The party teemed with political luminaries of the day. But
Donald Dawson, a one-time aide to Harry Truman, surveyed the

1

room and said: "Everyone likes John Rhodes, but most everyone here is a lobbyist."

If we weren't there, Rhodes would have been sorely disappointed—and a lot poorer. The President, the Vice-President and numbers of senators and congressmen were there, too. But they didn't pay to get in. They were there to attract the press and to impress the contingent of home folks who would return to Arizona more dedicated than ever to the re-election of John Rhodes. We were there to fatten his political treasure chest.

Next day, a colleague at the National Cable Television Association, for which I was then chief lobbyist, was horrified at an account in the Washington *Star* of my encounter with the President.

"How could you say that to the President of the United States?" he demanded.

"Say what?"

"That you were a . . . a lobbyist?" He spat the word as he might have if he were saying I was a Communist or a homosexual.

"Because I am a lobbyist," I said. He shrugged, opened his hands to the heavens, and walked out of my office.

Well, I said to myself, I *am* a lobbyist. I had been—officially, at least—for the previous twenty years. Before that, working in a law office or as an aide in Congress, I had been a lobbyist, too, though in a subtler way. Lobbying, by legal definition, means trying to influence legislation (for pay) on behalf of a special interest group. But hundreds of Washington lawyers, who frequently earn five times the money that professional lobbyists do, never register as lobbyists. They maintain, in their dealings with Congress and executive branch agencies, that they are merely legally representing their clients. And congressional aides lobby all the time on behalf of their boss's proposed legislation (as do White House aides)—and, often, their primary goal is not to improve the Republic but to enhance the re-election potential of the senators or representatives who employ them.

But, I conceded, *being* a lobbyist and *saying* you're one are different things. The term "lobbyist" does, after all, have a pejorative connotation. My mother has never introduced me to her friends as, "My son, the Lobbyist."

2

My son, the Washington Representative, maybe. Or the Legislative Consultant. Or the Government Relations Counsel. But never as the lobbyist.

I can't say that I blame her. Being a lobbyist has long been synonymous in the minds of many Americans with being a glorified pimp. You provide members of Congress, they think, with the Three B's of politics—Booze, Broads and Bribes.

A more conventional wisdom arose about a decade ago, largely through academic studies by the likes of Alexander Heard and the Brookings Institution, maintaining that lobbyists' money rarely influenced legislation; lobbyists were prized, instead, because they furnished vital information to congressmen on the points of view (supported by facts) of the myriad interests that make up the American Public.

As is conventional with most "conventional wisdom" about anything, both these ideas are partly wrong—and partly right.

A lobbyist can rarely influence a vote in Congress by plying members of Congress or their aides with whisky and wild women—at least, not directly. Nor is money to a politician ever openly considered a *quid pro quo* for previous or later support. But the relationship between money and favors from a lobbyist to a politician, and that politician's response to the lobbyist, can be so close that it is mere sophistry to suggest none exists.

And it is the rare lobbyist who represents the American Public. Even the so-called public interest lobbyists—environmentalists, consumerists and the like—don't work for free. The heads of several of these "public interest" associations earn at least as much money as senators and representatives. Take away their $45,000-plus annual salaries from some and see how hard they'd work against the oil industry or the SST.

The truth is that lobbyists generally represent the non-public interest—those individuals or businesses or groups that can afford a full-time professional whose job it is to develop access to those in power, and then to use that access to influence Congress or regulatory agencies or even the White House on behalf of whoever is paying the bill.

A not so noble profession, perhaps. But it clearly serves a key function insured by the First Amendment to the Constitution. It

3

permits the free assembly of people into self-serving organizations and provides them a direct pipeline into the halls of Congress. I have always believed that I play a role in the governmental process—and, unlike those who hypocritically profess to more noble callings like law (when, in fact, they lobby like the rest of us), I am unequivocal about what I do and for whom I'm doing it—and I'm a lawyer, too.

But power is Washington's primary product—and a lobbyist sells access to that power.

What made me among the more successful lobbyists in Washington for a generation is that, at any time, at least 90 of the 100 senators knew my name and face. The same went for about two-thirds of the 435 members of the House. And for Jack Kennedy. And Lyndon Johnson. Even the governor of Samoa.

There are, however, countless rip-off artists who call themselves lobbyists. Not only don't congressmen know who *they* are, they don't know the congressmen.

Take organized labor, in whose political vineyard I toiled for fifteen years as chief lobbyist for the Retail Clerks International Association. Weekly, some thirty-five labor lobbyists would meet under the chairmanship of Andrew Biemiller, a one-time congressman who for years has been the director of the legislative department (read: Chief Lobbyist) of the AFL-CIO. At these meetings it became clear to me that most of my colleagues, drawing high salaries to a man, hadn't the vaguest idea what most members of Congress looked like.

I took Biemiller aside one day.

"Andy," I said, "what do you think about conducting a test?"

"A test?" he asked. "What kind of test?"

"Oh, nothing complicated," I said with mock innocence. "Let's just hold up pictures of the members of Congress and have the lobbyists identify each one."

"You out of your goddam mind?" he blurted. "You know damn well half our people don't know who half the members are."

"Well, then, it seems to me it's time they learned. How the hell can they do any good in Congress if they can't even recognize the members when they pass them in the hallway?"

Biemiller's problem was that he believed the power of organ-

4

ized labor, of itself, would persuade members to vote labor's line. To some extent, he was right. Labor, perhaps more than any private force in American politics, could provide money and manpower for election compaigns. To get those indispensable goodies, congressmen used to have to walk that extra mile with labor and with George Meany, chief of the AFL-CIO. That meant voting not only for "gut" labor issues like minimum wage increases and against "anti-labor" laws like so-called "right to work," but it meant supporting the liberal issues so long espoused by Meany like civil rights and social welfare.

Times change—and except for Meany, few labor leaders want to push for government expansion in social programs like welfare. Union members have, in fact, become generally sharply conservative on issues like race and welfare. Congressmen are responding to that new conservatism. And a labor lobbyist who doesn't know a senator—his face, his family, his record—isn't going to have a prayer these days in getting that member to vote for a non-labor issue merely because it is supported by the leaders of organized labor. For one thing, new laws will severely limit the amounts of money labor can give directly to candidates. For another, as long as a congressman votes the labor line on clearly labor-oriented proposals, he will get all the volunteer help he needs with or without Gerorge Meany's or Andy Biemiller's say-so.

There are other rip-offs: Lawyers who charge up to $1,000 to see that a private immigration bill is introduced—knowing full well the bill will never be passed (some congressmen used to take up to half the fee for introducing such a measure and one congressman was indicted recently in a similar case). "Washington representatives" who charge high annual fees to non-Washington businesses or organizations to keep them posted on the "inside" developments in Washington—when, in reality, nearly all their "inside" information comes directly from the pages of the Washington *Post*, the *Kiplinger Magazine*, or any of a dozen or more sources of information readily available to the general public but which few know about. And the "legislative liaison" who charges hundreds of dollars to "arrange" a meeting

5

between a client and a senator—a meeting which, more often than not, could have been arranged by the constituent at no cost.

To some extent, nearly all lobbyists have been guilty of getting money from the gullible. It is incredible how naïve about the ways of Washington even the most sophisticated industrialists can be when they spend their working lives in New York, Chicago or Los Angeles, much less in Dubuque.

But for the greatest part of my working life, I have been what I consider a straightforward lobbyist both to my clients and to members of Congress, whom I must reach often enough to maintain those clients. The way I satisfy both wouldn't always enable me to qualify for nomination to sainthood. But there is very little about politics that is saintly. It may trouble some purists to recognize it, but the best way to reach politicians on the issues is by giving them money for campaigns, doing personal favors, and providing free manpower to help their re-elections. That gets their attention. And it keeps politicians on a short leash, making them more responsive to those whose efforts put them in power. Otherwise, an officeholder would be so far removed from his constituents as to threaten the reality of a representative democracy.

Before a lobbyist can get close enough to congressmen to influence them, he must not only meet those officeholders but he must build up a reservoir of confidence and trust. Meeting the members takes shoe-leather and patience. Winning them over, however, requires more; it takes proving your reliability and dependability.

One way that's done, I learned early in my career, was by "playing third base." That had nothing to do with baseball, though it involved a sort of national pastime, nonetheless.

2

BROOKS ROBINSON,
I WASN'T

"Playing third base" established me early among senators and congressmen as a reliable and trustworthy lobbyist. Brooks Robinson, I wasn't. But in that kind of game, anyone could play —anyone with discretion and ambition, that is.

The rules were simple. It usually started with a phone call, like the one I got in 1957 from an East Coast senator shortly after I began lobbying for the Retail Clerks International Association. The senator was friendly to the labor movement and he was among the first contacts I had made while making the rounds on Capitol Hill to tell members of Congress about my new job.

"Chuck," he said, "I'd like you to meet me for dinner tonight."

"Gee, Senator," I said, "I'd like to, but I think my wife has plans for us."

"Break them," he said curtly.

I was a bit miffed at his tone, but I was a relatively new kid on

7

the block and I didn't want to blow my job with needless heroics.

"Sure," I sighed after a moment.

"Eight o'clock at the Carroll Arms," he said. "Someone will meet you first and then I'll join you both a few minutes later."

I'm not a naïve person, but what happened when I got to the Carroll Arms—a now defunct Washington hotel near the Senate Office Building (and once a favorite watering hole for senators and their aides)—was, to say the least, surprising.

I was sipping a rob roy when a tall, lithe, beautiful brunette in her late twenties sidled up to me at the bar.

"Chuck Lipsen?" she asked.

"Yes," I answered, trying desperately to remember my marriage vows.

"I'm Gail. We were supposed to meet here and then wait for a friend."

It took a moment or two, but then the mists parted and the sun shone through the haze.

"Yes, indeed," I stammered, and led her to a table I had reserved for three.

We had about two drinks when the senator appeared.

"Chuck," he called out. "Chuck Lipsen! Good to see you."

He stood next to my chair and I rose to shake his hand. "Hi, Senator," I said. "May I introduce you to a friend of mine? This is Gail Smith." (I didn't know what her last name was, but I had realized it didn't make any difference—to me, anyway.)

"Well," the senator said. "So nice to meet you, too."

"Won't you join us?" I asked needlessly.

"That's very kind of you. I must spend another moment or two with one of my aides, but then I'd be happy to—if you're sure I won't be interrupting."

"Not at all," I assured. "We'd be delighted."

The conversation was loud enough to be noticed, if not heard word for word, above the chatter in the restaurant. The senator joined us, we all ordered dinner and, shortly after coffee, he excused himself. "I suppose you have to stay here a while longer," he said to me rather pointedly. I said I did.

"Too bad," he said. "I was going to offer you a ride home."

The hell he was. He lived in the District of Columbia while I had a house in a Maryland suburb. I began to sense what would happen next.

And it happened about ten minutes later. Gail tapped my arm and said, "I guess it's time for me to be going, too. I'll be back in a couple of hours, honey."

Then she left, too.

What happened, I later learned, was that she went directly to a room upstairs at the Carroll Arms, to which another lobbyist— one whom the senator didn't trust to hold his liquor in public— had already provided a key. I sat and swilled rob roys for a bit, took a walk around the block, came back and chatted with a couple of acquaintances of mine who had dropped in for a drink, and even did a crossword puzzle from the morning paper which a customer had obligingly left on the bar.

Gail returned, looking as lovely as she had a few hours before. "Hi, Chuck," she said. "Sorry I took so long in the ladies' room. Ready to go? Or would you like another drink?"

I was ready, I said. We left and I offered her a lift home. "No, thanks, honey," she said. "I've got cab fare."

I hailed a taxi and off she went. I would see her again in the years to come—sometimes with different senators. Gail was a pro. Sometimes the game would be played with a woman who worked in the office of a senator, with whom he was having a current affair. But it didn't matter. The game was always the same. Sometimes the hotel was different, the senators different, or the women different—and sometimes I used the time to take in a movie. But the game didn't change.

I always was rather philosophical about the role I played in these affairs.

I was hardly anyone to make judgments about the morals of others. Besides, I figured that I didn't care whether a senator liked to play cribbage or not. Why should I care if he liked to play house?

Perhaps it's rationalization. But I was young, ambitious and, like Ado Annie in *Oklahoma!* I just didn't know how to say "no" —at least to a United States senator.

Maybe I even did some good. Perhaps the guy felt better after

9

an evening with his girl friend. Maybe that way he'd feel better the next day, when he had to vote on issues like paying a higher minimum wage, or providing aid to education, or creating the Head Start program, or God knows what else that might make *other* people feel better.

And perhaps he was nicer to his wife that night than he otherwise might have been.

The "revelations" about Wayne Hays, John Kennedy, Lyndon Johnson—or even Martin Luther King—bore me. Time, it seems, makes the sexual interests of Grover Cleveland, Warren Harding or Franklin Roosevelt "acceptable." Would that Richard Nixon had succumbed to a similar human foible. Perhaps we would have been spared Watergate.

In any event, anyone who has no compassion for Hays, for example, is a cold fish, indeed. His "lady," Elizabeth Ray, worked hard to make a fool of him—and to profit from her success. Not type? I saw her hand beautifully typewritten letters to her one-time boss, Ken Gray of Illinois (no monk he), before she went to work for Hays. On several occasions, she asked me to help her find work on the side as "a party girl." We both knew what she meant. And she even approached Hays's secretary, Nina Wilson, for the private number (which Nina had) of Henry Kissinger. If she could reach him, she claimed, she could "get him in the sack in a week"—and that, she told Nina, would make a marvelous denouement for the "book" she was planning and later "wrote" and promoted. (It was interesting that while she appeared on television telling of her "pain" in being nationally spotlighted, she urged bookdealers to display her book prominently and appeared willingly at autograph-sales sessions.)

The truth is that while many women who work for congressmen may, in fact, have affairs with their bosses, it differs none at all from the head of National Widgets, Inc., who regularly sleeps with his secretary. The only difference is that in politics, the women drawn to congressmen are almost always workaholics. Liz Ray was a notable exception, at least as she tells it.

But so that no one thinks I'm a sexist, I should mention that I've played the role, with only slight variations, for two women members of Congress.

In one case, a lovely congresswoman who wanted to stay married simply wasn't satisfied with her husband as a lover. In the other case, it was clearly a situation in which the marriage was about to break up. These women would tell their husbands they were working late and had a meeting scheduled. They would instead meet their lovers, presumably in a discreetly out-of-the-way apartment, and would end the evening with me. For some reason, they both liked a little bar called The Place Where Louie Dwells. We'd have a nightcap and then I'd take them home. They would generally say that they met me after leaving the office—in the rare event that a question would be raised. Sure enough, one of the women still is married. The other is divorced.

As a member of Congress grows in stature—and, it follows, in visibility—the tactics change.

One group of three senators decided to rent an apartment (using my name, of course) in a building at which a restaurant called Club II now is located.

My job was simple. Once a month, I'd pay the rent from the money they would send me. Also, it was my job to keep it stocked with whisky, ice, cheese and crackers.

The members had a signal should there ever be any mix-up in the schedule for the apartment's use: the venetian blind visible from the street was to be kept pulled halfway up if the place were occupied.

One day, one of the three senators called me at my office—and he was fuming. "What the hell's going on at the apartment?" he demanded.

"What do you mean, Senator?" I asked.

"I've been down there three straight days with my girl friend," he fumed, "and I can't get in. One of my son-of-a-bitching colleagues has been there every damn afternoon."

I told him not to worry, that I'd take care of it.

"Well, see that you do. For Christ's sake, it's downright embarrassing."

I knew it was useless to telephone. The rule was that no one answered incoming calls. So I took a cab over to the apartment and, sure enough, the venetian blind was at half-mast. Cautiously, I climbed the stairs and rapped gently on the door.

11

"It's Chuck Lipsen," I called out. "I'm here with the delivery." No answer. I tried again. "It's Lipsen. It's only the delivery I promised." Still nothing. I put my ear to the door, but could hear no sound.

My heart skipped a beat. What if one of the men had been there, had a heart attack and collapsed, and the broad ran out of pure fear? What if a senator was dead in there? Oh, Christ, I thought, what would I do? How would I explain his presence there? Bad enough the guy was dead. Now his reputation would be ruined, to boot.

I tried the door. It was locked. I opened it with my key and stepped into the room.

"Hello," I called. "Anybody here?"

I walked toward the kitchen. Just then I heard a sound. I stepped quickly into the kitchen—just in time to see a mouse disappear through a crevice in the molding. Except for it, nothing was around.

I sighed, slumped on the couch and called one of the other senators who shared the apartment. I succeeded immediately.

"I was there a few days ago, Chuck," he explained. "But then my girl saw this mouse and like to peed in her pants. We got the hell out of there. I must have forgot to lower the blinds."

Well, that explained it. But I couldn't help being a little sore. "Jesus, Senator," I complained, "one of the other guys has been all over me. He thinks I screwed up the schedule."

"Tell the bastard to cool it," he answered. "Besides, it's your job to keep the place nice. Why don't you call the Orkin man or something and get that damn mouse outta there?"

I assured him I would, sighed and hung up the phone. You never win an argument with a senator, even if you're his social director.

With still others, the game gets more complex. One senator, a sometimes presidential candidate, regularly enjoyed the company of various girl friends. But his campaign travels not only made him widely recognizable but also kept him from being in one place long enough to make a permanent arrangement for a "safe house." But, bless him, his tastes were impeccable.

Once, when his current paramour was the wife of a wealthy

businessman, he telephoned me with a specific request. "Chuck," he said, "I'll be in Florida next week. I'd like you to arrange to get me a house. I'd like it to be large, nicely furnished, secluded and—oh, yes, this is important—it has to have a swimming pool that is completely private. We'd like to do a little skinny-dipping."

"And you need me to get you this next week?"

"Three days from now, actually. I'm counting on you."

I failed, and I don't know if the senator found his hideaway. We never discussed it, except once a few months later, when I told him that, by coincidence, I found a business acquaintance who had a house like that near Fort Lauderdale that could have been available only a week after the senator had wanted it.

"Good," he said with a straight face. "Next time I need one, you'll know where to look."

One way or another, the word spreads quickly on Capitol Hill that a particular individual, almost always a lobbyist, can be trusted to assist in, shall we say, delicate situations.

I suppose a lobbyist is often sought out by members of Congress in personal matters because the members know the lobbyist has nothing to gain and everything to lose if he is indiscreet. The seasoned lobbyist knows that personal favors won't be repaid through votes on bills that a member might oppose because of a deep, personal conviction or the political make-up of his constituency. But he does believe that on those issues which make scant political or conscientious difference to a congressman, the lobbyist will be remembered—and supported. And, once in a while, a member may even bend his politics or principles just a bit to help a lobbyist in need whom he, from time to time, has needed —and used—himself.

In the early 1960s, for example, Congress remained in session longer than had been anticipated and, as a result, many congressional wives already had returned to their husbands' home districts to prepare for the usual out-of-session get-togethers with constituents and local political leaders. One night, six congressmen whose wives had left town decided on a boys' night out.

At 3 A.M. next morning my telephone rang. My wife sleepily answered it and handed me the phone.

"Ish this Charlsh Lipshen?" an unfamiliar and obviously liquor-thickened voice asked.

"Yes. Who is this?"

"Never mind about that," he said, spacing his words drunkenly. "We're at police headquatersh and you're the man to get ush out."

"What is this, some kind of joke?"

"No. No joke. Wait a minute." He turned his face from the mouthpiece. "Offisher, would you please eshplain to the gennelman?"

A cop came on the phone and eshplained. He said he had taken six congressmen into custody after he had answered a complaint about a raucous party. The congressmen were there and were drunk.

"I took them in for their own protection," the policeman said apologetically. Indeed, Washington police never arrest members of Congress if they can possibly avoid doing so. Remember the case of Wilbur Mills, once one of the most influential members of the House? The night Fanne Foxe jumped into the Tidal Basin, Mills was drunk. A policeman led him away from the scene—and from a television cameraman. But he was recognized in a snatch of the film, anyway. That recognition led to the eventual disclosure of Mills's serious problem of alcoholism and led to his agreement to step aside as chairman of the House Ways and Means Committee. In the situation involving me, the police had spirited the six congressmen from the scene. One of them then gave them my name as someone trustworthy whom they could call and to whom they could safely be released.

"The gentleman you spoke to," the officer said, "didn't know you. One of the others gave him your name. But the one who called . . . well, sir, he was the most sober of the lot."

"God," I breathed. "I'd hate to see the rest of them."

"Yes, sir, but I'm afraid you're going to have to. They say you'll pick them up and get them home."

He told me the station they were at and gave me directions to it. I told him I'd be there shortly.

Jan, my wife, protested.

14

"Why do you have to go in the middle of the night?" she challenged. "Why don't they call a lawyer or something?"

"I am a lawyer, remember?"

"I don't mean a lobbying lawyer. I mean someone to take their case."

"Jan," I explained, "there is no case. The cops just want them off their hands. Besides, I know most of those guys. They've been helpful to me and I think they're calling me because they know I'll be helpful to them."

"And because you'll keep your mouth shut."

"That, too."

So off I went. As bad luck would have it, they lived all over the Washington metropolitan area. One lived in the District of Columbia, two in the Virginia suburbs, two in southeastern Maryland near Washington, and only one—the one who had suggested I be called in the first place—lived near to my own home. It was after 5 A.M. by the time I reached the home of the sixth congressman. He started to get out—and then, abruptly, stopped, turned back toward me with a quizzical expression on his face, and threw up over me, himself and half the front seat. I never got that smell out of the car and eventually had to sell it at a loss.

The man who had telephoned me—a congressman I had not met before—was a Southerner. Despite that, and his generally conservative political outlook, he showed his gratitude for that evening by frequently voting the labor line. It was not, he said to me often, that he owed it to me—although he felt that he owed me something. It was rather that after having given me several long hearings on the issues we were pushing, he had come to the honest view that most of our proposals were sound and fair for the vast majority of workers in the country.

There are more profound problems that lawmakers face, although public drunkenness will almost always ruin their political ambitions.

One such problem confronted a conservative senator, a Republican, in 1959. I called on him hoping he would oppose the Landrum-Griffin bill, a proposal feared by organized labor as the death knell to the labor movement (although it proved no such thing). Actually, I didn't really hope he would vote against the bill. Even some Democrats, normally friends of labor, weren't opposing Landrum-Griffin. It was designed, really, to limit the excesses of Jimmy Hoffa and the Teamsters Union (and, as it turned out, barely did that) and few congressmen could afford, at that time, to do anything that would seem supportive of Hoffa.

But I had a deep-seated belief that lobbyists—good ones—didn't stop lobbying after seeing their friends and supporters. Those were men and women who would vote for you come hell or high water—as long as you remembered them at election time. I believed you had to see your anticipated enemies as well. In a close vote, it was a switch of one or two votes from those members normally against you from which you could snatch victory from defeat. That philosophy caused more than one argument with my employers over the years—especially when it came to paying expense accounts which included lunches or dinners for congressmen or their top aides known to be on the wrong side of our political fence. But it paid off more than once.

In this particular case, the senator was a kind enough person to allow me to present my case. He listened courteously, but it was clear from the outset I was wasting my time—at least on this issue. I thought to myself that perhaps at some date in the future he would lean my way. But not this time, I thought.

Then the telephone rang. He scowled as if to say he had left instructions not to be disturbed. I thought he had done what so many senators and representatives do when they think they are obligated to be closeted with a lobbyist once in a while: they leave purposeful instructions to be interrupted by their secretaries with "an important call" after about five or ten minutes with his unwelcome guest.

As soon as the senator spoke into the phone, however, it was clear this was no brush-off call. In a moment, he seemed to go limp. Then he turned ashen. His forehead broke into a cold sweat and his hand trembled. I thought he might be having a heart attack. He placed a hand over the mouthpiece and looked up at me, his eyes wide with shock.

"My wife is on the phone," he said. "My daughter has slit her wrists."

16

I looked down at him and he stared back. I wasn't certain what, if anything, I was supposed to do. This was not the kind of situation your run-of-the-mill lobbyist encounters in his day-to-day work.

Then he broke the momentary silence.

"Help me," he pleaded.

There was no question in my mind that the man was going to be very sick if I didn't do something. Also, there was the not-so-little matter of his daughter. Somebody had better do something or God knows what might happen to her, if it hadn't already.

"Relax, Senator," I said, and took the receiver from him. I spoke to his wife, who was upset but in control of herself. I got her home address. Her daughter was lying on a bed now. She was losing blood but seemed in no immediate danger. I told her to stay with her daughter and leave the rest to me.

I phoned an ambulance company, a place where I knew the owner. I explained the situation and he agreed to keep his sirens off anywhere close to the senator's house so as not to attract needless attention.

Then I phoned the hospital where I had recommended she be taken. The hospital administrator also was a friend of mine. He knew that getting along in Washington (in terms, at least, of continued general support of federal aid to hospitals) sometimes meant going along with the wishes of VIPs. The wish in this case, I said, was absolute secrecy. The senator's personal physician would meet the ambulance at the hospital. No one else was to know the true identity of the patient. She was to be there under an assumed name which we agreed upon.

Next I had the senator give me his doctor's name and I called his office. I told the nurse at his office that it was an emergency and she put me directly through. When I told the doctor the arrangements, he was slightly annoyed. He didn't normally practice at the hospital I had chosen.

"Doctor," I said. "This is not only a matter of life and death. It's a matter of crucial sensitivity. I think you'd agree."

He said he did and was on his way.

Later I learned the girl had been on drugs and also had a recent abortion—illegal in those days. She felt estranged from her

17

parents and had tried to kill herself. Today the girl is happily married and has two children. Her father remains in the U. S. Senate. P.S. He voted against the Landrum-Griffin bill, and he still is one of the Republicans I usually can count on for support.

But after that incident—and even after lesser incidents, like the time my drunk friends called me, of all people, from the pokey—I often asked myself: "Why me?"

I realized that I could be depended on for discretion by virtue of my occupation, if not for my priestly face. But putting themselves in my hands like that, even at a moment when a daughter's life depended on it—well, that couldn't be explained merely by their counting on me to keep my mouth shut. It must have had something to do more directly with the relationship that evolves between a good lobbyist and a good congressman—a relationship in which each perceives that, but for the grace of happenstance, we might be filling one another's shoes. In fact, we often have. Many lobbyists are former congressmen. Others, like Roy Elson of the National Association of Broadcasters, have tried unsuccessfully for elective office before becoming lobbyists. Congressional aides often become either lobbyists or congressmen. While the difference between the two is seen by the public at large as being vast, we know better. We're political brothers under the skin, all in the same business but going at it from different directions. It is more than coincidence that most of us in top lobbying jobs (short of the super-lobbyists like ex-Congressman Frank Ikard of the American Petroleum Institute who earn in the six figures annually) are paid precisely the same as members of Congress. We all see ourselves as equal.

But in moments when I did something to help a senator or representative avoid serious trouble, or helped him through a personal crisis, I liked to believe there was more to being a lobbyist than "playing third base" or bending your elbow at the One Sixteen Club or the Democratic Club or the Capitol Hill Club or any other hangout of the politicians in Washington.

I liked to think there was something special about what I did. And while there's no place to go to school to learn lobbying, I knew I hadn't gotten where I was by accident. I had worked to be a good lobbyist. I had worked damned hard.

3

LOBBYING IN LUZON

Officially, I became a lobbyist on April 23, 1957. That's the day I formally registered with the Secretary of the Senate and with the Clerk of the House of Representatives, reporting that I was employed by the Retail Clerks International Association for the purpose of influencing legislation.

In reality, I think I've been a lobbyist all my life. If I could have, I would have lobbied to change our family name from Lipschitz. (Besides the scatalogical jokes, can you imagine meeting your girl friend's folks the first time? "Mom, Pop. Meet Lipschitz!") Fortunately, my father beat me to it. He changed his name to Lipsen shortly after he came to this country in 1922 and settled in Minneapolis three years before I was born.

I was still a preschooler when we moved to Des Moines and my father went broke in the meat-packing business. Next stop was Milwaukee, where my father sold horses and cattle on a free-lance basis. The Depression then took us to Madison, where he tried to make a living skinning calves and working on a WPA road project. But Morris Lipsen was lured by the land. He had grown up in a *shtetl* in czarist Russia, where Jews were prohibited from owning land. "Land are your roots," he would tell us. "Without land, you're nothing."

So we ended up with a small farm in a town of 800 called Mazomanie, near the capital of Madison, when I was a seventh-grader.

Almost immediately, I was faced with a problem that no amount of sweet, persuasive talk could solve, even though I was blessed with a golden tongue. During our first week in school, my brother, Hy, and I were beaten up by classmates who called us dirty Jews and kikes. My mother was planning to see the principal, but my father wouldn't hear of it. In his days in Des Moines, my father had befriended a fight promoter named Pinky George and one of his charges, Davie Day, a Jew who had changed his name from Daich. My father went to Madison next day and bought us boxing gloves and had us thrash at one another until we were bruised and exhausted. But the next week, when we were picked on again, the brothers Lipsen left four young bullies with black eyes and bloody noses.

I grew to six feet by the time I was in Mazomanie High School and was tailback on the school's football team. But I yearned for even more attention and became a kind of court jester. At an assembly before the big football game against Black Earth High, I rolled toilet paper down the center aisle and used it as a personal, ersatz red carpet. The principal was not amused and he forbade me from playing in the game.

I decided after that to quit high school. I wasn't a school hero any longer (they won the Black Earth game without me), and I was disturbed by people who assumed, because of my size, that I was a draft-dodger. I waited until I turned eighteen and then joined the Marines in the spring of 1943.

The Marines gave me another opportunity to be the center of attention—to myself, my family, my buddies—and to learn how to get things done with a little *sechel* and a lot of *chutzpah*, necessary attributes for lobbyists.

In fact, I learned a lot about lobbying from my years in the Marines.

I learned my first lesson before going to the front lines, however. At 147 pounds, I was boxing champ of my company and had won more than twenty fights in my weight class when I was matched against a marine named Tommie Tomlinson from Michigan. I was confident of victory—until twelve seconds into the first round, when Tomlinson broke my nose. Later, he tinned my ear. My only success was in landing a few jabs and managing to stay on my feet throughout the three-round fight. I learned from that experience to get to know my opposition before getting into a fight. I hadn't known, for example, that Tommie Tomlinson had been a Golden Glove finalist.

My boxing experience, which I had been developing ever since the seventh grade in Mazomanie, came in handy when I was crowded into the liberty ship *Frederick J. Lykes* with hundreds of other marines heading toward the Lingayen Gulf for the invasion of Luzon. During much of the trip, a sergeant in my unit, whom I'll call Greer, a 200-pound loudmouth, kept badgering me about keeping my rifle clean, keeping my boots properly laced and keeping my bunk straight. I wasn't certain why he was so bitchy until the day before we hit the island. With my buddies from my platoon as well as many others in the company listening in, he started pacing in front of me and spewing religious hatred.

"All the Jews are black marketeers," he said. "The *real* Americans are out fighting. Lipsen. why ain't you home making money like the rest of the Jews? I bet when we hit the beach you'll turn tail and run."

Everybody looked at me. With the eldest among us barely twenty-one, we only knew one way to prove manhood and courage. I had to show I had guts and that I wasn't afraid to back up my honor with my fists.

"You take that back, you son of a bitch!" I bellowed.

"Nobody calls me a son of a bitch, you kike bastard!"

With that, he belted me on the side of the head with a roundhouse right. I was dazed and my knees had buckled. But I put my head down like a battering ram and ran at him. I smashed him in the midsection with all my power. He doubled over and I caught him in the mouth with a left hook. He grabbed me by the throat and I pulled at his mouth with one hand while punching at his face wildly with the other. Grasping and flailing at each other, we rolled along the deck and tumbled through an open hatch into the hold below.

Just then, Lieutenant Rutecki rushed up and shouted at the yelling troops, "What the hell's going on here?"

Big Foot Thompson grinned sheepishly and said, "Sergeant Greer fell down the hold and Lipsen jumped in to help him."

"And," Rutecki fumed, peering down, "I suppose they accidentally collided and that's how come they're so bloody."

"Jeez," Thompson said, "you guessed it, Lieutenant."

Rutecki glared at the men. "Okay, break it up," he yelled. "And you guys get the hell out of there."

We climbed to the deck, bruised and disheveled. Rutecki fixed me with his dark eyes.

"Okay, Lipsen," he said. "This'll mean a court-martial."

"Why?" I asked.

He thought a moment. "For destroying government property."

"What property?"

"Sergeant Greer, that's what property."

Rutecki then looked at Greer. "Why'd he do it, Greer?" he asked.

"Do what, Lieutenant?" Greer asked through puffed lips.

"Fight with you, stupid!"

"He didn't, sir," Greer said firmly.

"He didn't . . . ? Well, how the hell did you get that way?"

"It's like Thompson said, sir. I fell down the hold."

Rutecki threw up his hands, whirled and strode away. Everyone let out a cheer.

"That was damn nice of you, Greer," I said. I stuck my hand out and he took it. He didn't apologize. He just looked at me and said, loudly enough for the rest of the men to hear, "Lipsen, you're the kind of guy I'd like to be in a foxhole with." I can't imagine a nobler display of eating crow than that.

My reputation for hell-for-leather bravery grew the next day, when I was first off our landing craft and first to hit the beach. I accepted the congratulations of the men (and Lieutenant Rutecki) for my leadership. In fact, I ran from the craft because I was seasick and was about to throw up.

Over the campaign, I received some minor leg wounds from grenade shrapnel, and I also contracted a case of malaria. I recovered, but not well enough to return to the front lines. So I concentrated on becoming head rooster of our camp.

To begin with, I was the only marine I knew who ever volunteered for KP duty. When I worked KP, I was near the food. When I was near the food, I knew that I would always get enough to eat. I was the best-fed marine in the Philippines. And I knew how to get those special extras that came along once in a blue moon. We were in Dagupan on the west coast of Luzon shortly before shipping out when an Army truck drove into our compound. The driver, a recent replacement and unfamiliar with Marine uniforms and insignia, mistook me in my fatigues for an Army warrant officer. He leaned out the window and called to me.

"Sir," he asked, "what do we do with the beer?"

I realized immediately we had struck gold. I instructed the driver and his mate to unload the beer and stack the cases in a nearby tent which I just happened to have been sharing with three other men. When the truck drove off, we all fell down laughing and the four of us practically knocked off one of the cases before nightfall. By then, the word had spread through the compound and we had a party until past midnight.

Next day a Marine captain came by to see me.

"Lipsen, I got a complaint from the Army this morning. Some officers are missing a truckload of beer. I understand you might know something about it."

I knew it was no use trying to bluff. I tried another tack. "Marines have to live off the land, sir," I said, straightening my back, "and, in my book, anything a marine can get from the Army isn't stealing."

"C'mon, Lipsen, don't pull that Corps crap with me. You don't have to." Then he smiled. "Okay. We'll split fifty-fifty. Half for you guys, half for the officers."

"Bullshit."

"What?"

"Sorry. Bullshit . . . *sir!*"

"What the hell do you mean by that?"

23

"I mean, sir, you get only ten cases."

"Ten cases? Do you realize I could run your ass in the brig for theft? Why the hell should I only get ten cases?"

"Captain, you can run me in the brig. You can take my corporal's stripes, you can court-martial me. But, Captain, if you take half the beer, the guys in this compound are gonna kill me. And then they're gonna kill you."

The captain thought a moment and then smiled again. "How about fifteen cases?" he asked.

"You got it," I said.

That was my second lesson in lobbying: you don't only have to know your opposition, you've got to be prepared to compromise.

Another lesson had been learned earlier, when I was based in Honolulu at a flight training school. I was up for sergeant and, because of my generally good work, I was invited to a reception one night for Colonel Charles Lindbergh, who was at the base for an inspection and a morale-boosting tour.

When Lindbergh entered the room, everyone was ordered to attention. I kept my seat. Our commanding officer averted an incident by ignoring me. I had heard that Lindbergh, on a prewar visit to Nazi Germany, had been decorated by Goering—and I thought he was a closet Nazi sympathizer. Next day, the CO removed my name from the promotion list. Some time later, it occurred to me I might have been wrong about Lindy. I thought he might have been sent by his government as much to scout the strength of the Luftwaffe as to show his personal interest in Hitler, and that he accepted the decoration to avoid a diplomatic blunder. New credo: Know the opposition, be prepared to compromise—and assume there are at least two sides to a story.

I learned my last lobbying lesson from the Marines after I was shipped back to the States. I was invited to go to Officer Candidate School—but that meant signing up for another four years. Despite my earlier bravado, I had had enough. One memory kept popping into my head. During my early combat days in the Philippines, I had been in a dugout with an officer named Captain Taylor. It was dusk, and the captain asked for a cigarette. I gave him one and, when I struck a match to light it, a bullet

24

whizzed past me and smashed the captain between the eyes. I had to stay with the body until dawn.

But if I did not go to OCS, I would be shipped back overseas and likely would see combat again. I decided to solve my dilemma by going into Los Angeles alone and getting dead drunk. I woke up in a flophouse sometime next day with more than a hangover. I was alternately shivering and sweating. It was another bout with malaria. I reported to a nearby naval hospital and was admitted. A nurse named Lieutenant Bubick let me cry on her shoulder about my problem. I didn't want to go back. Okay. I was afraid. I had done my share, after all. I had a Purple Heart and five battle stars. But I didn't want to mortgage the next four years of my life to the Marine Corps. I was twenty years old, I wasn't even a high school graduate, and somewhere along the line I was going to have to learn something about making a living.

"Listen," Lieutenant Bubick would say, "it's not going to help anything if you just lie there and worry. Relax. Things'll work out, you'll see."

One morning she brought a newspaper to my bedside. I looked at the headline and couldn't quite comprehend it.

"What does it mean?" I asked.

"It's the atom bomb," she said. "The paper says it's the most powerful weapon ever invented. We dropped it on Japan."

I read the story. There had been reports of massive destruction and President Truman had threatened to drop it again if Japan didn't surrender. He said the reason for its use was to avoid the necessity—and the anticipated bloodshed—of an American invasion of the Japanese mainland.

Tears came to my eyes. I must confess they were not tears of concern only for the tens of thousands of Japanese casualties, nor of course, did I know then about the dangers of radioactive fallout. They were tears of relief. This new bomb might end the war. And that meant I might not have to go back; there would be no invasion.

"I think you're going to make it," Nurse Bubick said. "I think you're going to go home."

I lay back and savored her words. Home. Mazomanie. The land. The folks. My two brothers and two sisters.

That was the last lesson about being a lobbyist that I would learn in the Marines: you could study your opponent, you could develop imaginative and reasonable compromises, you could burn the midnight oil to digest all facets of an argument. But it could all go right down the drain if you didn't have a little luck.

4

I FIND A WIFE
AND WASHINGTON

It took me about a week before I became restless in Mazomanie. I spent most of my time in nearby Madison seeing old friends and dating occasionally at the University of Wisconsin. My social contacts were limited there, though. Most of the students I would meet dropped me as a friend soon after they found out I wasn't even a high school graduate. I thought they were snobs. But, at the same time, I realized I couldn't hope for much out of life without an education. But I was already twenty, and I didn't think I could do anything about it.

Then I met Janice Greenberg, a seventeen-year-old freshman from Glen Cove, New York. She was pretty and petite, but nearly as gregarious and outspoken as I was. And as impetuous.

On our second date, I asked her to marry me.

"I love you, too," she told me, "and I'd love to say 'yes.'"

"Then why don't you?"

"For one thing," she said, "my father's a dyed-in-the-wool East-

27

erner. He wouldn't hear of me marrying anybody west of East Orange, New Jersey. But for another thing . . . well . . ."

" 'Well' what?"

"I was just going to say that, well, maybe it would be easier for my father to accept you if . . ." She broke off again.

"What were you going to say? If I weren't a poor farm boy? Just because he owns a department store and I've got cow shit all over my shoes?"

"Calm down, Chuck," Jan said. "It's not the way you think it is. He'll like you and so will my mother. But maybe for your own good—and for our future—you should think about finishing high school and coming to the university."

"I've thought about it."

"You ought to. Not just for me or my folks. For yourself."

"Oh, Janice, I know that. But I'm too old. I'm too damn old!"

"You're never too old. You're just twenty. Why don't you give it a try?"

"I'll think about it," I promised.

I asked my parents about the idea that night and they were all for it. Next to the land, education was my father's greatest love—again, because he had so little of it in his own life.

Next day, I called on the principal at Mazomanie High, the same man who had kept me out of the big football game more than three years before.

"This hurts me more than it's going to hurt you," I said, "but I want to get back into high school and get my diploma."

The principal was understanding. Despite my age and size, he decided to let me attend classes for a few weeks. There'd been a war, he said, and the younger students would be able to adjust to an older person being in the school. In reality, he just wanted to see if I was serious about my studies. When he was convinced, he gave me a high school equivalency examination. I passed and was awarded my diploma and I immediately applied for admission to the university.

By the time I was admitted to the freshman class, Jan was a sophomore. By that time, I had been bitten by two bugs. The first was to become an agent of the FBI. I still recalled the thrill of anticipation I felt each week as a boy when a radio program called "The FBI in Peace and War" was about to come on. These days, that sort of thing is regarded as rank propaganda promulgated by J. Edgar Hoover. But to me, it was the stuff of great dreams. And it gave me the incentive I needed to get a college degree. Not only that, but I figured that to be an agent of the FBI, I ought to get a law degree as well.

The second bug was called love. I decided I didn't want to wait until Janice and I had graduated from college. I wanted to get married as soon as possible. One of Janice's sorority sisters, more as a joke than anything else, dared us to get married if we were so all-fired eager to.

"What do you say, Jan?" I asked. "Why don't we take her up on that?"

Jan thought a moment. Then her eyes sparkled and her mouth broke into a grin. "Why not?"

We got into my pickup truck and headed out of state (we couldn't get married in Wisconsin without a waiting period). We found a justice of the peace in Dubuque, Iowa. But on the way back to the campus, Jan began complaining of chills and fever. I drove her directly to the infirmary. She had flu. I canceled the hotel room that I had reserved. It was ten days before we had our wedding night.

We moved into a small, two-room flat over a tavern in downtown Madison. In season, I helped my father on the farm. I sold shoes in a local store for six dollars a day. Later, my father gave us enough to open a small butcher shop, which Jan worked with me. Almost nine months to the day after we were married (or, rather, after our marriage was consummated), our first daughter, Sandra, was born. She slept in a crib next to our bed.

I rushed to classes between work and Jan would leave Sandra with my parents during the day so she could attend her classes. We both tried to study in the apartment at night but, when I was lucky, Jan told me she didn't need me at home and I could slip off to the library. At night, after study, we tried to get to sleep despite the nickelodeon in the tavern below rinky-tinking "Put another nickel in . . ." until well past midnight. But even when we drifted off, Sandra's habit of clunking me on the head with her baby bottle would quickly waken me.

29

Somehow, both of us finished and won our degrees and I promptly enrolled in law school. Meanwhile, Jan, who was now nineteen, was elected chairman of the membership committee of the Wisconsin State Democratic Party. While it was clearly an honor, we both recognized that, at that time, the Democratic Party was so small it practically could have conducted a statewide caucus in a telephone booth. Inevitably, though, Jan drew me into politics, too. It was too tempting to ignore, even though I was up to my eyeballs in torts and claims. We were like pioneers, trying to start what amounted to a new political party as far as Wisconsin was concerned—and there was plenty of room at the top for young and politically ambitious, if inexperienced, people.

So, while I was still a law student, I ran for alderman of the eighth ward of Madison. I lost by twelve votes. The winner, Ivan Nestigen, went on to become mayor of Madison—and an undersecretary of the Department of Health, Education and Welfare under President Kennedy.

I continued working in politics, squeezing in what activity I could between work, classes, nickelodeons and Sandra's deadly aim. But my first foray into the national scene came through sheer coincidence.

Two of my law professors summoned me one afternoon.

"You were in the Marines, weren't you?" one of them asked.

I told them I had been. They explained that two journalists, Ronald May and Jack Anderson (now a famous syndicated columnist), were writing a book about Senator Joseph McCarthy of Wisconsin. McCarthy's political star was on the rise then and the professors frankly feared him and his harsh tactics. They were helping May and Anderson to gather material for the book.

"I don't like the son of a bitch, either," I said, "but how can I help?"

The professors, Jack DeWitte and Carl Runge, looked at me for a moment.

"It's like this," DeWitte said evenly. "McCarthy was in the Marines. He was a captain. Now, *he* says . . ." DeWitte paused. "I want to emphasize here that this is what McCarthy claims. It may be perfectly true."

"But," I said, "you're hoping whatever it is won't be true."

"Exactly. To come to the point, McCarthy says when he was in the Marines, he had been wounded. In fact, he says he took enough shrapnel in his leg to leave him with his limp. May and Anderson have reason to believe it isn't true. Needless to say, they'd like to catch McCarthy in a lie, especially concerning his war record. It might put a little chink in his super-patriotic armor."

"I understand," I said. "But I still don't see how I can help you."

DeWitte triangulated his hands by pressing his fingertips together and said carefully: "You wouldn't have any old war buddies still active in the Marines, would you?"

"Well, yes. In fact, a bunch of the guys have re-upped. One or two . . ." Suddenly, it came to me. "I think I *can* be of some help, sir."

"Good, Lipsen," DeWitte said. "Let me know if you get anything."

As fortune would have it, one of my Marine friends had been assigned to the Pentagon—and worked, of all places, in the records division. It didn't take much cajoling to get what I wanted.

"Sure, I'll do it," my friend answered when I asked if he could slip out a copy of McCarthy's war record and make a copy for me. "As far as I'm concerned, every one of these creeps in Washington is a goddam armchair hero."

I didn't argue with him. This was one time when I welcomed military distaste for civilian authority, and conquered my own distaste for impinging on someone's privacy.

A few days later, I received a copy of McCarthy's war records. I promptly put the results into a brief but revealing report which I passed along to my law professors.

McCarthy had been hospitalized while he was in the Marines, all right. But it wasn't because of shrapnel or any other perceptible war wound. It seems that when McCarthy was aboard a troopship which was passing the equator, his mates wanted to initiate him into the Shellback Club.

His troops grabbed him and started carrying him forward and pulling off his clothes for the traditional dunking in the sea when someone—especially an officer—crossed the equator for the first time. McCarthy scuffled with them and, unfortunately, slipped on the deck. He yelled in pain. He had injured his hip and was shipped back to a hospital as soon as practicable. Despite the best efforts of military physicians, McCarthy retained a limp— serious enough to keep him from ever having to go to the front during the war. That was McCarthy's famous "war wound."

Needless to say, all of us were gleeful, including the Washington journalists to whom the information was passed (and who later utilized it in their book *McCarthy: The Man and the Ism*). The word that I had been responsible for this little coup quickly spread among our small Wisconsin Democratic Party with the result that I won greater respect—and responsibility—in the state organization.

The incident became a turning point for me in 1950, when the party leaders gathered at the Pfister Hotel in Milwaukee for the traditional Jefferson-Jackson Day dinner. Senator Estes Kefauver was the principal speaker for the evening and my sister, Esther, who was chairman of the dinner arrangements, was seated next to him at the dais. Esther, always a booster (and now, as Esther Coopersmith, one of Washington's best-known political hostesses), made certain that Kefauver learned of my role in providing the Congress and the country with one of the few good laughs it ever was to have about Joe McCarthy.

After the dinner, Esther introduced me to the senator. "I like what you did about McCarthy," Kefauver said. "Have you ever thought about coming to work in Washington?"

I told him I had.

"Well, if you come, you be sure to look me up. Maybe we can use a good investigator like you on my crime committee."

A new bug had bitten me there and then. No longer did I crave the FBI. Washington was, as young people came to say, where it was at. And, true to form, I wanted to be at the center of the action.

I finished law school later that year, packed my small family and our few belongings into the pickup truck, and headed East to action, fame and fortune. When we arrived, I promptly learned that none was easily available.

I called Kefauver's office and was given an appointment. The grin of anticipation I wore when I entered his office dissolved as soon as he started talking.

"Chuck," he said in his resonant drawl, "I'm afraid I have nothing available right at the moment on the crime committee."

I asked him if he knew of anything else available on Capitol Hill, but he shook his head. "I'm afraid I don't," he said. "But I'll be sure to keep you in mind when I hear of anything."

I didn't believe him. But, in fact, he would play an important role in my life and political involvement in the not too distant future.

For the moment, though, I was in a strange, new town which I had never even visited before—and I was without a job. Fortunately, my sister had preceded me to Washington with visions of national influence similar to my own. She, too, was unable to land a congressional job, so she had joined a trade association called the National Association for Railway Progress. She was working for a man named William Merriam (who later became the top Washington lobbyist for ITT and was deeply enmeshed in the still unresolved Dita Beard incident involving influence peddling for favorable antitrust treatment from the Nixon administration).

I wouldn't hear of the possibility of working for a lobby. It was, I told Esther, beneath me. Besides, I didn't want to get mixed up with a bunch of sordid characters—especially any espousing conservative or business-oriented causes.

Esther was bright enough not to argue with me, except to assure me that she didn't mingle with sordid people, either.

"Okay," I said, "I shouldn't have sounded off. But I want something different, Esther. I want to work on the Hill."

She promised me she'd see what she could do. A few days later, she gave me a list of names of congressmen and congressional aides whom she knew from the contacts she made for the railway association. I started making the rounds, but I had no luck.

"Have you tried Olin Johnston yet?" Esther asked me one evening. Johnston was a senator from South Carolina.

"No. Hell, Esther," I said, "I told you I don't want to work for

33

some goddam reactionary, much less a southern peckerwood to boot."

"Chuck," she answered, "you've got a lot to learn about this town. For one thing, Johnston is no peckerwood. He's a bright, courtly gentleman. For another thing, he's no reactionary. As a matter of fact, he's one of the best friends organized labor has got."

"From South Carolina?" I said in disbelief. "With all those textile mills down there trying to keep the unions out?"

"The textile mills don't elect senators," Esther said. "The people do."

"Then why are all the rest of the Southerners anti-labor?"

"Because they get their campaign money from the mill owners."

"Well, then, what about Johnston?"

"He gets his money from labor."

"And wins anyway?"

"And wins anyway. I told you he was bright. He sells his position to the people. He makes them understand that unions will mean more money in their pockets—and people like that."

I agreed to see Johnston—or rather, one of his aides. I was still reluctant after that chat, especially when I was told there might be an opening for a young lawyer on one of Johnston's subcommittees. It was the manpower policy subcommittee of the Post Office and Civil Service Committee. It didn't sound earthshaking.

"Why don't you call the chief counsel of the subcommittee?" the Johnston aide said. "Here, I'll jot down his name and number for you."

I took the slip of paper, mumbled my thanks and left the office. In the hallway, I glanced at the name he had written: Melvin Purvis. Melvin Purvis?

I quickly stuck my head back into the office. "Sorry," I said. "But is that *the* Melvin Purvis?"

"The one and only," I was told.

"Thanks," I said, and I was on my way to see him.

Melvin Purvis. That was a name that I had read about and thought about for years. He had become one of the heroes of my

34

youthful fancy. Purvis was the man who had caught the notorious John Dillinger while he was an FBI agent. It had been his feats that were in large part responsible for my earlier ambition to become an agent myself.

When I met Purvis, I wasn't disappointed. He seemed tough, quick and aggressive—but friendly. I told him that my sister was acquainted with Johnston and that I was certain Senator Kefauver would provide a recommendation for me. Purvis checked me out, arranged a meeting for me with Senator Johnston (who, I had to confess, seemed everything Esther had said he was), and I was promptly hired at $4,800 a year.

I learned that manpower policy was hardly a bore. It related to efforts by President Truman, Senator Johnston and the Democratic majority in Congress to try to minimize unemployment through a variety of government training and subsidy programs. It was controversial, especially as Senator McCarthy was rising to enormous national influence through, among other things, his insistence that government was riddled with Communists hired because of policies too broad to insure careful screening.

One result was that Representative Jamie Whitten of Mississippi sponsored an amendment designed to cut sharply the number of government jobs. Whitten, like many members of Congress, believed that government was too bureaucratically fat —which it may well have been then as it clearly is today. But the alternative was to increase unemployment at a time when Senator Johnston and others believed it would be economically— and humanly—disastrous to do so.

After it passed, studying the Whitten Amendment and developing arguments for its repeal became the chief occupation in my new work. By December, six months after I had joined the subcommittee staff, I completed what I believed was a first-rate report that could be the basis for repealing the amendment despite its growing popularity in Congress. I left the report for delivery to Purvis and took a holiday with Jan back in Wisconsin.

When I returned, I felt refreshed and was ready to do battle against the amendment. But on my first day at the office, Purvis called me in. In my dreams, I had never imagined he could look quite as menacing as he did that morning.

35

"I'm dissatisfied with your work," he said bluntly. "I'm going to have to fire you."

His words made my knees feel suddenly weak.

"Fire me? Mr. Purvis, for God's sake, why?"

"For one thing," he said, "you haven't even written a single report on any of your assignments. I gave you six months. But you should have finished something by now. You haven't."

"I haven't written a report?" I said with justifiable amazement. "Mr. Purvis, I've already written two—including that long job on the Whitten Amendment. In fact, I was kind of proud . . ."

"The Whitten report?" Purvis interjected. "You've written that?"

"Well, sure. I left it to be retyped and delivered to you so you'd have a chance to go over it before I got back. Then we could go into any changes . . ."

"You left it here before your vacation?"

"Yes. Why, is something wrong?"

He thought a moment. "Don't worry about it just now," he said. "In the meantime, forget what I just said. Go back to work on your other projects and I'll get back to you."

"Does this mean I won't be fired?"

"Yes. At least," he added, "not now."

I was still shaky. I didn't know what had disturbed Purvis but, whatever it was, I was certain to know before long. And I had no idea whether that meant I would still have a job or be back on the streets—this time, without a recommendation from anyone.

Two days later, Purvis called me back into his office.

"Remember how you bitched about your salary last month?" he asked.

"I remember," I said. It was when I had discovered that while I was being paid $4,800, two other young law school graduates were receiving $6,000 apiece. One had been from the Yale Law School, the other from Harvard Law. I was disturbed not only by the discrimination against a Wisconsin graduate; I was also troubled that these men both were bachelors and still made $1,200 a year more than I did.

"Well," Purvis said, "you're getting a raise—to $6,000."

"Gee, Mr. Purvis," I exclaimed, "that's great. That's just great news. I can't believe it."

"Believe it," he said.

I sat looking at him for a moment and then dropped my eyes.

"Go ahead," he said. "Ask."

"Okay. How come one minute I'm fired and the next minute I'm getting a big raise?"

"I never thought you'd ask," he said, smiling. "Luckily for you, my boy, you're working for an old sleuth. I checked into what had happened to those reports you said you had written but that I had never received."

"You never received them?"

"Well, that's not exactly true. I had received them. But they had been written by one of your Ivy League chums."

"The hell they were," I fumed. "I worked day and night on that Whitten report."

"I'm sure you did. But when I received them, they didn't have your name on them. In a word, my boy, they were stolen from you. Purloined. Plagiarized."

"For God's sake," I sputtered. "How?"

"Elementary, my dear Lipsen. You left them in the secretary's box at night for retyping. But before she came to work in the morning, they were removed from the box—and your name was removed from the reports. The nice man who tried to screw you is currently out of work."

From that day, I would have supported Melvin Purvis for anything—FBI director, President or even God. The experience made me redouble my efforts for Purvis and for Johnston. Before long, I had become Purvis's right-hand man and by the fall of 1952, my salary had risen to $8,000 a year—despite our failure to repeal the Whitten Amendment.

But in the 1952 elections, General Eisenhower's victory at the polls pulled enough Republicans into office to give the GOP a Senate majority for the first time in twenty years. And that meant disaster for me.

The reason was that committee chairmen in the Senate are selected from the majority party. Chairmen, in turn, hire those men and women they want to staff jobs on the committees they chair. I was a Democrat working under a Democratic chairman. The new committee chairman was Senator William Langer of North Dakota. While a handful of former staffers were retained despite the switch in party control, I was not among them. But it wasn't Langer's doing. It was mine. I quit.

"You're a good worker," Langer told me the day I resigned. "I wish you'd stay."

"I wish I would, too," I said. "I'm not looking forward to being out of work."

"Then why?" he asked.

"I've asked myself the same question. I suppose it's that I've just become so closely identified with the Democrats. If I worked for you, it would blur my political identity."

"And if you don't," he said, "it'll do worse things to your pocketbook. Anyway"—he smiled—"I do have one or two people of my own that can do the job, too, you know."

I knew. That was patronage and, while it cost me my job, I couldn't complain about it. It was part of how the spoils system worked. If you backed the right horse, you won your bet. If you supported the right candidate, there was gold at the end of that rainbow, too. These days, that wouldn't have happened. The rules of Congress were changed to assure that the minority party (almost always, that meant the Republicans) would have staff representation on every committee and subcommittee. That year, 1952, would have been one of the few times that Democrats would have benefited from the change. But at that time, it was losers weepers down the line.

I had no job lined up and couldn't think where to start. I even dallied with the notion of returning to Wisconsin and running for Congress. I still had enough political connections there to mount a reasonably effective—and possibly victorious—primary campaign. But the chances of a Democrat winning the general election were slim, at best. Besides, I would have to go home, open up a law practice and somehow try to earn a living while gearing up for the race two years away. If I lost, which I knew was probable, I was hoping the publicity would at least enhance my law practice.

But the thought of returning to Mazomanie or Madison to concentrate on cases involving automobile accidents, minor thefts or occasional divorces dimmed the brief candle of political ambition that had lighted my mind.

I couldn't decide what to do with my life. I had spoken to Senator Johnston, but he had only suggested working for a trade association.

"You mean become a lobbyist?" I asked.

"Why not?"

"That's not the kind of thing I had in mind when I came to Washington," I said. "I want to work on the Hill . . ."

"Lobbyists do."

". . . and help write laws . . ."

"God knows, lobbyists do that, too."

". . . and help influence the passage of those laws."

"Chuck," Johnston said evenly, "you've worked with me for two years. Haven't you ever dealt with lobbyists?"

"I suppose so."

"You know you have. Whether they've been from the Civil Service Commission or from labor unions or from the businesses who were opposed to federal wage increases."

"Yes, but they were representing special interests."

"And what do you call a congressional district? A congressman representing a particular district is representing a special interest, too. An Oklahoma congressman is for the oil interests. A representative from North Carolina is for tobacco. A Kansas man is for wheat and the farmers. And a senator from New York, where the liberals are, is against segregation, while a senator from my state and the rest of the South, where Negroes live in great numbers, is for it."

I had to admit that Johnston made a persuasive argument. Whether they were from concerned agencies of the executive branch, private industry, labor or other organizations, or even from Congress itself, it seemed that people with an interest in a piece of legislation—whether they thought it might make them richer, poorer or get them re-elected—were, to a great extent, lobbyists.

I pondered what he had said but before I had a chance to do

anything about it, I received a telephone call at my office only days before I was scheduled to vacate it.

"Chuck Lipsen?" a voice with a nasal whine asked.

"This is he."

"Chuck, this is Joe McCarthy. What're you doing for lunch?"

5

McCARTHY FINDS ME—
AND MORRIS

I didn't know what to make of it. Why would Joe McCarthy call
me? I had seen him occasionally during the previous two years
and he had spoken to me cordially enough—particularly since he
had learned that I had been the original source of the information about the way he received his "war wound." I knew he had
been angered by it and, characteristically, he had denied the
story as "a Communist-inspired damned lie." He knew full well
that the chances of his military records becoming public were
slim, if not impossible. And even if they had, he would have denied them as forgeries. After all, it was unlikely that the military
would publicly comment on the validity of any published report
about someone's presumably private records—especially since
McCarthy had begun to make some ominous noises about investigating the loyalty of some top officials in the Pentagon, State
Department and other areas of government.

Suddenly, I felt my stomach flip-flop. It couldn't be, could it,
that McCarthy was planning some sort of "exposé" of congres-

sional employees? Especially those of us who were active in Democratic causes and, ergo, liberal movements? Practically anyone left of Attila the Hun seemed to be labeled a Communist in those days. I searched my memory for acquaintances who were of questionable political background. I remembered that at the university a number of my political chums styled themselves as socialists. But that was hardly unusual for college students— especially at Wisconsin, the home of Bob La Follette the Progressive, and the city of Milwaukee, which had a Socialist mayor for as long as anyone could remember. Surely, Joe McCarthy wouldn't get after me for that. Or would he?

It was with a good deal of trepidation—but with even greater curiosity—that I walked over to the Carroll Arms and was shown to a restaurant table where I was to await Senator Joseph McCarthy.

From the stir at the entrance to the restaurant, I knew he had arrived. McCarthy was a garrulous, gregarious man despite his public image as dark and satanic (or, to his supporters, fiery and evangelical). He was almost a caricature of what had come to be known as "ordinary Americans" in one generation, "plain, hardworking citizens" in another, and the "silent majority" in yet another. He was ordinary in intelligence, plain in his looks and demeanor—and, like Richard M. Nixon with his "Pumpkin Papers" of a few years before—he knew how to energize an apparent majority with frightening specters of enemies within.

But, unlike Nixon, McCarthy abhorred being alone. He sought out people and he possessed that certain magic shared by so many politicians that made people seek him out, too, no matter how unattractive he grew to so many Americans who watched him on television or read of him on the editorial pages.

He broke from the klatch of people who had surrounded him, caught my eye, grinned and waved, and then limped toward the table.

We exchanged pleasantries and ordered drinks—martinis, at his insistence—the first of four or five rounds we were to consume that afternoon. In fact, I can't recall if we ever ordered lunch.

He must have noticed I was a bit fidgety, perhaps even nervous, because he laughed unexpectedly and reached across the table to clap me on the arm.

"C'mon, Chuck, relax," he said. "There's nothing wrong in this town with a Democrat and a Republican breaking bread together. Look, I don't usually beat around the bush, so I'll come right to the point. I'm chairing this new investigations committee you've read about. I want you to be my chief counsel."

You could have knocked me over with a red herring.

"You want *me*? After what I did to *you*?"

"That bullshit about my leg? Christ, I don't care about crap like that."

I knew that wasn't true. Friends of mine who worked with McCarthy on Senate committees at the time had told me he was livid—and once even offered to show two fellow senators his shrapnel scars while the three were standing shoulder to shoulder before a Senate urinal. His colleagues declined the offer.

"Anyway," he continued, "that's over and done. Let's bury the hatchet, huh? You're from Wisconsin, like I am. All that happened to you is that some pinkos at the university got hold of you and warped your mind." His laugh crackled through the restaurant.

"But it's crazy, Senator," I said. "I'm a Democrat."

"I used to be a Democrat, too, you know. It beats having the clap." He roared at his own joke again. Then he leaned toward me and narrowed his eyes as if he really meant business.

"Listen to me. You're from Wisconsin and that's important. But I want a Democrat and, to be honest, I want a Jew."

"Why?"

"I want someone in that spot who won't seem to be a political hatchet man for me. I want him to be seen as a liberal. Then people will have more confidence in the committee's work."

"And a Jewish Democrat would be considered a liberal?"

"Absolutely."

He paused for a moment.

"And it pays $16,000."

I tried not to choke on my drink. Even now, a salary of $16,000 is something above the poverty level. In 1952—especially

43

to a young man then earning $8,000—it sounded like the contents of Fort Knox.

McCarthy could see he was reaching me. But he didn't stop there.

"This job will put you in the spotlight," he said. "You'll be respected and—mark my words—you'll be feared. You'll have more power than two-thirds of the senators."

"I'm not sure that I want to be thought of as a modern-day Torquemada," I said.

"You don't have to worry about that. I'll be the heavy. I'll get better press that way, anyway. And I want this thing to become the number-one business of Congress as far as the public is concerned."

"You really believe this stuff about Communists in State and the Pentagon?"

"And elsewhere. Don't be naïve, Chuck. Look at the Hiss thing. You think the Russians are stupid? This Cold War can be a hot war at any moment. They got the A-bomb from us, didn't they? We lost China to the Reds, didn't we? Where do you suppose they get the stuff that puts them on an equal footing with us?"

At the time, I allowed myself to share the incredibly chauvinistic belief of most Americans that we had "lost" China to Mao because of our failure to support Chiang sufficiently. And I believed that American secrets were stolen from the United States and became the basis for Soviet success in developing nuclear devices of their own. While I still believe there were—and are—foreign intelligence agents in our country, I don't think they constitute a serious threat to our security.

Nonetheless, I thought that despite McCarthy's scare tactics, he must be on the right track. Perhaps I could be of help. Maybe I could persuade him to take greater care during his investigation than he had earlier in spraying his accusations around as if he were seeding a lawn. Still, if I cast my lot with McCarthy, it would brand me from then on as a Democrat who helped a Republican—and a damned unpopular one, at that—heap suspicion upon numerous government officials and private citizens,

44

many of whom were bound to be wrongly implicated through association.

McCarthy must have seen my consternation, because he retreated from the argument about the dire necessity for his committee to flush Communists from the bushes and, instead, threw his Sunday punch.

"If all goes well, Chuck," he said in a confidential tone, "you might even be in a position after this thing is over to run against Wiley."

My head jerked up and I looked him in the eyes. Alexander Wiley was the senior senator from Wisconsin—and, like McCarthy, a Republican.

"Your name'll become a household word back in the state—and," he added with meaning, "I'll support you."

"You can't mean that, Senator," I said in disbelief. "You'd support me—a Democrat—against Wiley?"

"I'd support you," he said. "Even a Democrat—if he did a job for me."

We talked some more and drank some more until both of us were high. Whether it was the gin, the pay he offered me, the promise of fame, the chance to run for the Senate or all of the above, I found myself liking Joe McCarthy.

By the time I got home, I had all but decided to accept the job. I couldn't wait to tell Jan the news. She might as well have poured a pail of water over my head.

"You can't work for him," she said evenly.

"Well, why the hell not?" I demanded.

"He's against everything we've ever believed in and worked for in Wisconsin," she said. "Besides, he's a dangerous man."

"Dangerous man?" I parroted. "Dangerous man? I'll tell you who's a dangerous man. Me. I'm out of a job. I've got a wife and a kid and a second kid on the way. I'll probably go rob a bank or something. And, Jan," I added, pleading now, "with this job, I can go straight to the top."

She was silent for what seemed like minutes.

"I'll go along . . ."

"Great!" I exclaimed.

". . . on one condition."

"What's that?" I asked.

"You'll call your father first."

"What for?" I asked.

"Because," she replied, "I want you to call him and ask what he thinks. He's always helped you when you were in a jam. And you've always valued his advice."

"But this is different," I insisted. "This is politics. Pop doesn't know anything about politics."

"He knows about people. And he knows right from wrong."

I agreed to talk it over with my father, but I couldn't wait until morning. I phoned right away.

My father listened quietly as I rambled on excitedly about the job offer. I told him everything except the possibility of running for the Senate. I figured that might be pressing too hard.

When I finished, I thought I could guess what he would say. I suppose in my heart of hearts, I wanted him to say it—because I suppose I had made my own mind up as well but wanted and needed some support for my weakening conscience.

"Take the job," he said.

"What?" I thought the connection was bad.

"Take the job," he repeated.

"Pop, you *want* me to take it?"

"Yes. But," he added, "don't bother to come back to Wisconsin or to my house."

Before I could say anything, his voice rose and his emotions rose with it.

"That *momser!*" he cried. "That bastard! He's nothing but a killer! Another Hitler, he is! Another Haman!"

Then he cooled down a few degrees. "Look," he said, "you go practice law, teach, do anything. Make what you can. I'll send you money. I'll take care of you. Just don't work for that bastard. You don't need to do that."

"Okay, Pop," I said soothingly. "Okay. You're right. Really. I agree with you and Jan agrees with you. I'll make out. I'll find something."

Next day, I went back to see Senator Johnston.

"I couldn't agree more with your wife and your father," he said. "If you were to take a job under that man, it would destroy everything I believed about you. Don't be a mugwump."

46

"What's that?" I asked.

"Hell," he said, "I don't know. It sounds good. I use it to describe a guy who sticks his mug on one side of the fence and his wump on the other."

(Actually, as I later learned, a mugwump was a Republican who failed to support his party in 1884, when Democrat Grover Cleveland nosed out the GOP's James G. Blaine for President. Later, it came to mean anyone who was a political maverick. I suppose the expression would have fit me, a Democrat, had I become McCarthy's confederate.)

I told him I had been considering what he had told me about becoming a lobbyist. He gave me names of a few friends in trade associations, most of whom I knew myself, and told me to feel free to use him as a reference. He wished me good luck and I left. But before going out to try to find work, I had one last chore at the Senate.

I headed to the Senate floor. The Senate was in session and I had been told by his office that Senator McCarthy was there to make a speech in support of the proposed appropriation for his new investigations committee. I sent a note through a page to the senator, asking to see him. He came out promptly.

"I've made up my mind, Senator," I said. "I appreciate it—but, no thanks."

He was diffident. He pursed his lips thoughtfully.

"You're making a big mistake," he said. "I could make you a big man, you know."

"I know," I said. "But somehow, I guess I don't think I want to make it that way."

We shook hands. "Nothing personal, I hope," he said.

"Not at all," I lied.

Not much later, McCarthy hired a man named Roy Cohn as his counsel. Though Cohn wasn't from Wisconsin, McCarthy had gotten his Democrat and Jew. Cohn's name became the household word that McCarthy had promised. And he remains a successful lawyer in New York.

He became a big man, all right—but not in the sense I would have wanted. I decided that for me, it was best to keep my mug and my wump on the same side of the fence.

6

WORLD WITHOUT
LOBBYING ... AMEN?

Folklore has it that the oldest profession is prostitution. I always thought it was lobbying. The serpent in the Garden of Eden talked Eve into trying the apple from the Tree of Knowledge by successfully portraying knowledge as a virtue rather than the vice that God had made it out to be.

For his efforts, the serpent was punished by God by being forced from then on to crawl on his belly in the dust.

To much of the public mind, lobbyists belong alongside the serpents. But was the serpent the villain that the opening chapters of Genesis depict? Was he evil for opening the minds of men and women to knowledge? Or was God merely offended because, in his own words, knowledge made man "become as one of us . . . ?"

It is true that lobbyists often present as virtues those notions widely assumed to be vices. It is also true that they buttress their arguments with pledges of support to helpful congressmen of the Three M's—Money, Manpower and Materials—for their next political campaigns. But a widely held distaste for their clients, their views or their willingness to support politicians who, in turn, have supported them don't mean their causes are wrong or evil.

The acid test for justice in America has always come when the accused have been unpopular, powerless people. It takes little courage for a jury to acquit the rich and the strong. The Richard Nixons of the world receive pardons before they've even been charged with a crime. The Richard Kleindiensts are charged with obscure misdemeanors even when they have committed felonies like lying under oath to Senate committees (and then are handed suspended sentences—and even praise from the sentencing judges). And the high-level, confessed or convicted architects of the Watergate crimes spend a few months in the comfortable dormitories of prison farms. Yet the minor-league burglars who touched off the Watergate revelations—the so-called Cubans, who honestly believed they were working for the CIA on a mission to protect their country from subversives— each spent well over a year in prison and would be there yet had it not been for the compassionate recognition of Judge John Sirica of the gross inequalities involved.

For the lobbyist, there is, more often than not, the paradox of representing a well-financed cause or group whose goals are nonetheless either widely unpopular or strongly opposed by factions frequently as well endowed. But it is usually a matter of opinion and little else when someone decides that what a lobbyist is after constitutes seeking special privilege rather than wanting to redress a grievance.

For instance, oil company lobbyists are assumed to be the minions of special interests because they fought for years— successfully until recently—for oil depletion allowances that kept their employers from paying taxes at the same rates as other corporations. But we are beginning to understand in the United States at last that oil reserves are, indeed, finite and that there is an end to the black gold after all. And oil companies which have spent tens of millions of dollars searching for new pools to tap from the land, the sea or from shale are suddenly being cheered

49

for their efforts. It used to be that they were condemned for greedily seeking greater sources of revenue.

I am not for a moment suggesting there are no bad lobbyists and no ill-conceived and profiteering causes. Of course there are, just as there are bad doctors, overbearing priests and ministers, crooked politicians, usurious moneylenders, shady retailers and cruel Little League baseball coaches.

But to assume that representing special interests is a stain on the American system is to display ignorance of what that system is about.

In *The Federalist* papers, James Madison recognized "the mischiefs of faction." But to remove the causes that led to special interests, he wrote, would require destroying liberty and homogenizing opinion—creating a world characterized chillingly in later years by George Orwell in *1984*.

With the development of industry, lobbying grew to protect the interests of the new class of manufacturers and landholders. In the early 1800s, Alexander Hamilton helped organize the Philadelphia Society for the Protection of National Industry to lobby for a high tariff, among other things. Other groups organized to draw up legislative goals. In the 1830s, the great Senator Daniel Webster openly accepted more than $30,000 from the Bank of the United States to fight the efforts of President Andrew Jackson to break its power by removing federal deposits from it.

In the 1850s, Presidents like Pierce and Buchanan were no match in Congress for industrial barons like Samuel Colt whose chief lobbyist, Alexander Hay, presented expensive revolvers to friendly congressmen—and, in at least one case, $10,000 (a much grander sum then than it is today) to a member for his help in getting Colt an extension bill for patents. Gun lobbies have been a source of political largesse ever since—and have been incredibly successful in fighting gun control laws despite the national traumas of assassinations and attempted assassinations of the past decade.

Thurlow Weed, who variously represented textile mills (to try to lower import duties on wool) and railroads (for land-grant bills), was probably the first major lobbyist who succeeded because he added political savvy to payoffs. Weed didn't think it wise (or possible) to buy enough congressmen regularly enough to support successfully controversial bills to protect or enhance industry and big business. So he found other valuable ways to boost friendly politicians' fortunes. Through his friend Horace Greeley, he helped some get favorable press stories; with others, he guided them to rich and influential contacts to make profitable investments. Most important, he was a shrewd political adviser and organizer; he even played an important role in organizing the Republican Party, which was to elect its first president, Abraham Lincoln, in 1860.

The nation's leading lobbyist after the Civil War was Samuel Ward, characterized by James Deakin in a book about lobbyists as "The King of the Lobbyists." The brother of Julia Ward Howe (who wrote "The Battle Hymn of the Republic"), he had a pedigree dating back to one of the framers of the Constitution. He was, Deakins wrote, "a mathematical prodigy, a Latin scholar, a poet, a gourmet, an accomplished pianist and guitarist, a wit and a *bon vivant*."

He was a friend to Presidents and poets, and one of his early key jobs during the Civil War was, for $12,000 a year, to "court, woo and charm Congressmen, especially Democrats prone to oppose the war," according to Ward's own letters. During a Senate investigation of a mail subsidy action he was retained to support and push through Congress, he insisted he had paid no bribes; rather, he said, he merely befriended congressmen and entertained them at dinner.

"Talleyrand," he explained, "says that diplomacy is assisted by good dinners. At good dinners people do not talk shop, but they give people a right, perhaps, to ask a gentleman a civil question and get a civil answer."

While Ward may never have directly bribed anyone to win his victories, he did resort to tactics that, like throwing dinner parties for congressmen, are still in vogue, with variations, today. One of the most important things a lobbyist does, if he can't persuade a congressman to vote his way, is to prevent him from voting at all. Usually, getting a congressman "to take a walk" can mean winning an important committee vote. Recently, I represented the National Cable Television Association in a fight to minimize the effects of a new copyright law on cable television operators. I had persuaded the cable TV industry to compromise by accepting a proposal to pay a small percentage of their revenues to the copyright-holders of those programs they aired. The Senate committee considering the proposal was split, with about half the members pushing for our industry to pay an even higher copyright fee; the motion picture industry was supporting the higher percentage because that would add to its profits.

One vote I had been counting on was that of Senator Birch Bayh of Indiana. I had known and supported Bayh for years. Both my wife and my sister, Esther, had been key workers in 1964, when Bayh, then a freshman senator eager to make a national name, was chairman of "Young Citizens for Johnson." Jan and Esther arranged for a series of "Young Citizens" barbecues across the country which had been resounding successes financially for President Johnson—and for the personal exposure of Senator Bayh.

On the morning of the vote, however, I was shocked to learn from one of Bayh's aides that the senator planned to vote against me and for the movie industry. Bayh was also a close friend of Jack Valenti, the one-time Johnson aide, who is president of the Motion Picture Association of America. Bayh was also planning to run for President—and presidential candidates thrive on having movie stars available to draw paying customers into campaign fund-raising events.

I wasn't angry at Bayh. Valenti could be of great help to him in the campaign. And I wasn't angry at Valenti. Not only was he taking the best position for his industry on that issue, but he supported the cable business when it came to its efforts to expand pay-cable television (which would also benefit the motion picture business).

Besides, having a "name" at a fund-raiser is imperative. Representative Thomas (Tip) O'Neill of Massachusetts, now the Speaker of the House, drew 7,500 people to a picnic in his honor at which, by no mere coincidence, Carl Yastrzemski of the Boston Red Sox was in attendance. "You suppose," O'Neill asked me rhetorically, "that more than a hundred and fifty people would have come just to see Tip O'Neill?"

"Probably a few more than that, Tip," I said.

"Maybe. But anyhow, you can bet the Red Sox management will be on my doorstep to try to get TV blackouts for sports events in the area."

Tit for tat. That's the way it was played.

Anyway, my problem was to keep Bayh from going to the committee at all. His aide told me he would be leaving for Indiana shortly after the committee vote on my bill.

"What's the chance," I asked carefully, "of him catching an earlier plane?"

"There isn't one," he answered laconically.

"Maybe you can just tell him he's late. Look, don't even tell him the reason. Just get him the hell out of here. It won't kill him if he misses the vote. And he owes me."

He thought a moment. "I'll see what I can do," he promised.

I thanked him. But I didn't have time to wait and make certain that Bayh would walk. For even if he did, I still lacked one vote to assure that our position would win in committee. I needed to make sure of one more vote for our side—and I knew one waverer who was close to me.

It was Senator Hugh Scott of Pennsylvania, the Republican leader of the Senate. Scott would not return to the Senate after 1976. I didn't know that then, but I suspected it. Scott had, unfortunately, been used in the midst of the early revelations about Watergate. John Dean, once President Nixon's White House counsel, was implicating Nixon in the scandal. Scott had been shown some carefully edited transcripts of Dean's tape-recorded conversations with the President. He had been assured by Alexander Haig, then Nixon's chief of staff, that they were accurate. But, sadly, Scott didn't use his instinctive political wisdom and he failed to question the validity of the transcripts, although nearly anyone with savvy had by that time concluded, at least privately, that Nixon must have been neck-deep in the Watergate cover-up. Still, Scott had publicly denounced Dean as a liar —and was later embarrassed by the truth.

I also had not known at the time that Scott would be accused of taking a virtual $10,000-a-year retainer, à la Daniel Webster, from the Gulf Oil Corporation. But I knew that Scott was no

53

stranger to lobbyists or their favors. I had personally seen to it that in 1970, when he had run for the Senate, he had significant financial support from organized labor. Whatever one might think of Hugh Scott, he was, during his Senate career, one of the most consistent supporters of legislation that benefited working men and minority groups. Without his stalwart help, liberals would have lost greatly needed Republican votes to make the civil rights hopes of the early 1960s become realities.

I checked Scott's office and was told he was in a meeting of the Senate Foreign Relations Committee. It was a closed meeting to hear Secretary of State Henry Kissinger report on the negotiations leading to the Sinai accord between Egypt and Israel.

"Can he leave for a few minutes," I asked his top aide, "to run over to the committee vote on the copyright bill?"

"You've got to be out of your mind," the aide shot back. "The whole Middle East can go up at any minute if this damn treaty isn't approved. And Scott is carrying the ball for the Administration on this."

"It won't take long," I pleaded.

"No way," he said. "Half that committee wants to shoot Kissinger down and the senator has to defend . . ."

"Get his ass out of there!" I shouted uncharacteristically. "You go tell him I need him for one fucking minute, and if I don't get him, I'm dead and out of a job. You tell him he owes me that!"

"Cool it, Chuck," he soothed. "I'll give it a try. But don't count on anything."

"Okay, okay," I said. "Listen, I'm sorry. But it is important."

I paced the halls outside the committee room. No Bayh. That was good. But no Scott, either. Come on, I begged of Scott mentally. Be good to me. And around the corner of the corridor he came, puffing his pipe, walking his clipped duck-walk.

"Senator," I said excitedly, "I can't tell you how much I appreciate this."

"Lipsen," he said, "you don't even know how I'm going to vote."

Oh, Christ! I had been so intent on getting him to the meeting, I had forgotten to make sure he would come down on my side. He saw me blanch—and then he smiled.

54

"Take it easy," he said. "I wouldn't have left Kissinger if I was going against you."

I felt like kneeling and kissing his hand. Bayh never showed up—and we won by a single vote.

Getting people to show up for a close vote, or keeping those away who are against you, is a stratagem that goes back at least to the days of Sam Ward. In a letter from Ward to his friend Henry Wadsworth Longfellow, he told this anecdote:

"When I see you again I will tell you how a client, eager to prevent the arrival at a committee of a certain member before it should adjourn, offered me $5,000 to accomplish his purpose, which I did, by having his boots mislaid while I smoked a cigar and consoled him until they would be found at 11:45! I had the satisfaction of a good laugh, a good fee in my pocket, and of having prevented a conspiracy." The "conspiracy" probably referred to a bill Ward opposed himself. Ward once said that "the profession of lobbying is not commendable. But I have endeavored to make it respectable by avoiding all measures without merit."

The point is that most measures, as Ward well knew, have merit to someone's interest—and it is merely a matter of opinion as to what is meritorious and what isn't.

Men like Thurlow Weed and Samuel Ward began lifting the business of lobbying from the crass practices of buying votes to a more subtle, respectable level.

But the line between the two is a thin one. Bribery cases continue, although in the post-Watergate era they seem to have gotten out of hand. Take the case in Maryland of Governor Marvin Mandel. Even Mandel's political opponents grant that he is perhaps the best governor the state has ever had. Not only did he live up to his campaign promises of not imposing a major tax increase, but his administration has been responsible for several key programmatic innovations, especially in education. And he balances the state's budget, year-in, year-out. But in a convoluted indictment, the Justice Department accused him of granting favors to his political friends in return for financial gains— gains that amounted to some $15,000 over more than a year.

It should be understood that granting favors to his friends was

55

not at issue. It isn't a crime. And there was nothing wrong in Mandel receiving the business interests he got from those same friends. There was nothing illegal in that, either. What the government sought to prove—and what would indeed be a crime if committed—was that Mandel took the $15,000 specifically in return for the favors he granted—a *quid pro quo*.

Now, these same friends of Mandel had been responsible for raising nearly one million dollars for his campaign for governor in 1974. Is it unusual, then, that he would give legal favors to these same men? And would he require that they do him additional service before he would respond to their requests for governmental help? And, finally, is there anything wrong with helping your friends when to do so is legal? If you don't help your friends, whom do you help?

It is supposed to be somehow immoral for someone who scratches your back to expect his scratched in return. I have never understood the outrage that this principle of politics regularly excites among so-called public interest groups. They are as effective as any industrial lobby in raising money and manpower for those candidates who have supported their positions on pending legislation. And if that's not returning favor for favor, I don't know what is. The difference, perhaps, is that groups that organize around an ideological flag, as opposed to those of us who work for labor or business, expect and demand 100 per cent loyalty from congressmen. That a vote on a particular issue might spell political defeat for a congressman seems not to matter at all.

In 1968, when Birch Bayh was running for his second term in the Senate, he attended a meeting in Indiana of supporters of Senator Eugene McCarthy of Minnesota, the anti-war candidate. Bayh, at that time, had been something of a hawk on Vietnam. The group shouted and berated Bayh for his stand on the war. With tears starting in his eyes, Bayh reminded the people they had been the backbone of his support six years earlier, when he had come from nowhere to upset Republican Senator Homer Capehart. They jeered.

Bayh told them how he had risked his popularity by strongly supporting civil rights measures. He reminded them of how he had ramrodded a bill to provide relief to the people of his state and others who had earlier been ravaged by floods and tornadoes. And he reminded them of his work to pass the Twenty-fifth Amendment to the Constitution to see to it there would always be a Vice-President—an amendment which proved a few years later to be the steadying rudder of the nation in that nightmarish period when both a President and Vice-President were forced to resign their offices.

Finally, Representative Andrew Jacobs, Jr., stood up and quieted the group, which had threatened not only to drop from the rolls of Bayh supporters, but to support actively his Republican opponent (who was much more hawkish on the war than Bayh) out of pure spite.

"I have here in my pocket," Jacobs said, "a statement in which I was planning tonight to endorse the candidacy of Eugene McCarthy." The audience cheered.

"But I swear to you that I'll tear this up right here and now if you people continue denouncing Birch Bayh the way you have. You have no right to expect that he will be in total agreement with you on each and every issue. He has been a great senator— better than people who act as you do deserve."

In the end, Bayh modified his position on Vietnam (and eventually strongly opposed continuing the war). But most of those people still did not support Bayh because he was not, in the words of one of them, "pure enough on Vietnam." It is that kind of purism that is a danger to politics in America.

Critics used to smirk at Lyndon Johnson's efforts at consensus government. But I have yet to discern a more realistic and beneficial notion in a large, heterogeneous country like ours than compromise.

Lobbying is the business of presenting one of at least two points of view on a serious political question facing a segment of society. A lobbyist wants his client's position to prevail. But he knows almost at the outset that he cannot hope to win a whole loaf. So, in battle with lobbyists from the other side, he seeks compromise. And without compromise, it is difficult to see how our nation, its economy and its people could long survive.

James Madison was right. A nation which eschews factionalism really cannot abide freedom. Freedom means factionalism. Factionalism means compromise. Compromise requires lawmakers to hear opposing views. The lobbyist is the spokesman for those views. Those who would say a reflexive "amen" to a world without lobbyists had better know the freedoms they would thus sacrifice on the altar of what they perceive to be incorruptible government.

7

I TELL IT
TO THE JUDGE

It was a bleak winter. First, I tried my father's suggestion and called on a dozen or so law firms. But the first question they would ask was how much business I could bring to the firm. The answer was simple. None. I had developed numerous political contacts, all right, but I hadn't a single prospective client.

And none of my political contacts seemed to have any jobs available, either. With another politically displaced person, Robert Dunphy (later sergeant-at-arms of the U. S. Senate), I went to see Jiggs Donahue. Donahue, a powerfully influential Democrat, then was the commissioner of roads for the District of Columbia. He, too, would soon be replaced when President Eisenhower was inaugurated. In those pre-home rule days, Presidents appointed the D.C. government and Mr. Eisenhower would be putting Republicans in top bureaucratic jobs.

We all accepted the system gracefully. It hadn't been many years before that Alben Barkley, then a senator from Kentucky, had told a Democratic National Convention his definition of the word bureaucrat: "A bureaucrat," he intoned, "is a Democrat who's got a job that some Republican wants." So it was, after twenty years in the wilderness, Republicans would become bureaucrats once again.

Donahue, however, arranged for Dunphy and me to see a man in the D.C. highway department whom he thought might be in the market for two bright, young men.

The man was affable enough when he welcomed us, but soon made it plain he had nothing to offer in the way of employment.

"Try to see it from my side," he said apologetically. "I'm trying to keep my job despite the new Administration coming in. If I start hiring guys like you who've been active in Democratic politics, my head would roll."

"I suppose you're right," I sighed.

"I'm sorry. I'm afraid I haven't got a thing—unless, of course, you'd be willing to be line painters."

"Line painters?" Dunphy asked.

"Yes. You know. The guys who paint lines down the middle of the streets."

We both laughed.

"Well," I said, getting up, "thanks anyway."

"Okay. If you change your minds, give me a call."

"Change our minds about what?" I asked.

"About being line painters," he said.

"You're serious, aren't you?" I asked.

"Sure," he said.

"I'll tell you what," I said, my Marine blood starting to boil, "why don't we start by painting a line down your middle—just for practice."

"Listen," he said, startled and stepping back, "I didn't mean any offense. I figured you were hard up and at least it's steady work."

I took a step toward him but Dunphy grabbed my arm and I allowed him to lead me out of the office and back onto the street.

"Can you imagine the nerve of that son of a bitch?" I fumed.

"Calm down," Dunphy consoled. "It just goes to show that when you're out, you're out. And there isn't a hell of a lot you can do about it."

60

Nonetheless, I decided to return to Donahue's office and tell him what had happened.

"Christ," he breathed. "I'm sorry, Chuck. I had no idea anyone would stoop to that."

"More precisely," I said, "ask *us* to stoop to that—literally."

If he thought it was funny, he didn't laugh. I perceived that his own loss of influence had embarrassed him more than it had either Dunphy or me.

Donahue, however, arranged an appointment for me with another of his contacts. He was Andrew Federline, a lawyer who worked near the Capitol and who specialized in highway safety laws. He had a generally good, thriving one-man business representing states and localities before congressional committees dealing with federal safety proposals and with appropriate government agencies responsible for federal highway programs. As it turned out, Federline's business was growing quickly enough, especially with talk about a major, new federal highway program, to prompt him to offer me a job as his assistant at $10,000 a year. Donahue had come through, after all.

For a while, I did general legal research for Federline. Soon, however, he suggested I consider "branching out."

He explained that friends of his in the direct mail business were looking for someone to lobby against proposed increases in bulk mail rates.

"I got them interested in you," he said.

"Me? How come?"

"Don't be naïve, Chuck," he said. "You used to be a top staff man on the Post Office and Civil Service Committee. If you don't have the contacts there, nobody does."

"Gee, Andy," I said, "I don't know if I could do something like that."

"Like what?" he asked.

"You know. Pull strings with people I know."

"Who do you want to pull strings with?" he asked facetiously. "People you *don't* know?"

"You know what I mean," I mumbled.

"Sure, I do. But I don't think you know what *I* mean. You're not going to get these people to do anything illegal or immoral.

61

You're going to simply tell them the story of the direct mail industry. Like how much it contributes to the economy. Like how many people are employed because of it. And, last but hardly least, just how many postmen are kept employed simply because they're needed to deliver junk mail."

"The way you put it," I said thoughtfully, "sounds reasonable."

"And remunerative," he added.

"How much?" I said, my interest growing.

"Your share will come to two hundred dollars a month."

That did it.

In fairness to my new clients, I pointed out to them that much of the leadership of the committee and most of the staffers had changed. Of course, Senator Johnston still was among the ranking Democrats and Senator Langer, though a Republican, knew me and liked me.

But I pointed out that I thought that much of the work would be with the staff members and there were a raft of new faces who had come in with the Republicans.

Still, I was successful in my first lobbying effort. For some two years, while representing the direct mail industry, I kept the committee from passing any significant price increases. My work was something we call "negative legislation"—lobbying to keep any new law from passing. It is often the greatest service lobbyists can perform for a client, whether it is the gun lobby succeeding in bottling up any severe regulations on handguns or rifles, the oil lobby maintaining depletion allowances, or organized labor trying to limit control over its political involvements.

The experience also made clear to me that the lobbyist who slights or ignores key staff members who work directly for senators and representatives, or who work for those committees on which the members serve, will have minimum or short-term success at best.

Some lobbyists spend all their time—and their clients' money —wooing a few congressmen who hold leadership positions on committees pertinent to their work. Others cozy up to White House officials, including, sometimes, the President.

In the latter case, there is no doubt that, for example, every time William Whyte of U. S. Steel played golf with President

Ford, he so deeply impressed his employers that his job was secured for at least another year and his salary jumped along with it. And several top businessmen serving as state-level finance chairmen to the campaign to re-elect Gerald Ford in 1976 were influential in persuading the White House and the Justice Department to withdraw initial support for new antitrust laws that would have prevented mergers until all pending opposing litigation had been completed.

But only a few people are fortunate enough to have the ear of any given President. And when that sort of lightning strikes, it has done so for one of two reasons: either those with access to a President are very rich and have been instrumental in financing his political campaigns, or they had known the man who got to be President when he was a member of Congress.

The latter reason, of course, grows out of solid work done by a lobbyist in earlier years. In Whyte's case, he got to know Jerry Ford when Ford was a rising star in the House of Representatives. So when Ford, through a series of almost incredible circumstances, became President, it gave Whyte entrée to the White House that he perhaps never believed could occur. But when President Carter took office, Whyte was back where he started in terms of his ability to persuade lawmakers to support or oppose legislation affecting his industry. If he had not maintained his association with senators, representatives and their staff members, he would have become almost worthless as a lobbyist.

As for the rich who gain entrance to—and influence with—Presidents, their days are numbered. For one thing, only a few of these people are rich enough to support in significant terms more than one candidate at a time. Thus they have to choose the right horse to ride. If they lose, they have no more influence on the White House than Archie Bunker. For another, new limitations on campaign contributions make them much less important than they used to be to prospective Presidents.

A top aide to one senator explains it this way: "Under the new laws," he says, "the federal government provides $250 in matching funds for each contribution of $250 or more. An individual is limited to giving $1,000 to a particular candidate in a particular election. If a man gives a candidate a check for $1,000, the government adds its $250. That makes a total of $1,250. But suppose you get that guy to give you a check for $250. Then he gets his wife and each of his two kids to write you checks for $250 apiece. The government matches each of those checks with $250. So while he—or, rather, his family—still has given you $1,000 in sum, you pick up a total of $2,000 instead of $1,250."

What that means, the aide says, is that candidates go hunting more for middle-class people, who were virtually ignored in previous elections by candidates' finance chairmen. Not only may they be able to afford a contribution of $250, but they tend to be more politically active and are successful, therefore, in finding many other people to make similarly small contributions.

So the fat cats, formerly an inevitable and powerful part of any candidate's campaign, are no longer sought after with the verve they once inspired among those with political ambition. Some, like W. Clement Stone for conservatives and Stewart Mott for liberals, will still be allowed to spend millions, if they wish, for a candidate as long as they do it without the co-operation of their choices. But only a few people with great wealth choose to spend much of it on politics.

While the way to a congressman's heart is nonetheless still through his pocketbook, though in smaller doses these days, the way to his office is through his staff. Those of us who could rarely buy our way in but who spent our time and our luncheon expense accounts on a congressman's administrative or legislative assistant have suddenly found ourselves in a much stronger position on Capitol Hill than ever before.

Those who depended on giving big contributions to lard a congressman's campaign treasury but who rarely became close either to the members themselves or to their top aides are now lobbyists trying to come in from the cold.

Courting staff members is a basic to successful lobbying. For one thing, registered lobbyists alone outnumber congressmen five to one. When you add the legion of unregistered lawyers, constituents who own businesses, industrialists who call on members whose committees are considering legislation affecting their livelihoods, the congressmen are forced to spend more than half their average working day seeing people with real or imagined problems. Adding to the difficulty is that while every member of Congress has one vote, some votes are more equal than others.

In some cases, a single member can control the outcome of a piece of legislation. Wilbur Mills, when he chaired the House Ways and Means Committee, single-handedly devised major tax bills, received an automatic stamp of approval from the rest of the committee, prevented the bills from being amended once they reached the full House for a vote, and generally persuaded the Senate to avoid major changes. When Senator Pat McNamara was chairman of the Senate Public Works Committee, he appointed himself chairman of each and every subcommittee. No federally financed bridge or dam was constructed in the country without his personal approval.

Therefore, if your business with Congress concerned taxes or pork barrel projects, one had to see Mills or McNamara. Sometimes, it was easier to see the Pope. The only direct way either to see these men or to make certain a message got through to them was to have developed a relationship with members of their committee staffs. More often than not, these staff members were and are youthful but highly intelligent experts whose advice and counsel are indispensable to their committee chairmen. If you knew these people and had dealt with them from time to time even when you weren't looking for a particular legislative favor, you could be sure they would hear your story when there was a problem. They might not always come through for you—but at least they would listen. Without a hearing, there is no way to prevent adverse legislation and no way to add something to a bill of benefit to a client.

Working with staff members of the Post Office and Civil Service Committee, I kept direct mail costs down. They were persuaded that the manpower reductions in the Post Office Department that would be necessitated should the industry be curtailed would not be worth the added revenue of sharp increases in direct mail costs. And while some constituents screamed louder than ever about the amounts of junk mail they were receiving (and that first-class mail was costing them more than ever), most people just went along simply tossing out the unwanted mail

65

and didn't bother to blame their congressmen for the inconvenience.

After nearly a year working as Federline's assistant, I thought it was time to become more seriously—and, potentially, more profitably—involved in lobbying. Both through my work for the Young Democrats of Washington, D.C., and my efforts for the direct mail industry, my contacts in Congress were growing daily. As vice-president and national committeeman of the local YDs, I began moving regularly in circles that included most of the top senators and representatives in Washington. And their aides were my colleagues in the organization.

I moved to a job, paying $12,000 a year, at the National Paint, Varnish and Lacquer Association, headed by a retired Army officer, Brigadier General Joseph F. Battley. The problem was simple and direct. A group in Congress was trying to push through legislation requiring that certain indoor paints carry on their labels the word "poison," its symbol (the skull and crossbones) and a warning to keep the paint away from children.

The industry believed that would be disastrous for its product, though later experience with the tobacco industry, forced to carry warnings on its products and in its advertising, indicated that people will buy them anyway—even in growing numbers.

Unlike the tobacco industry then, however, or the American Medical Association in later years in the fight against Medicare, we were willing to compromise. We came up with an alternative plan we believed would meet reasonable fears without putting paint in the same public category as arsenic. So we proposed a new label requirement for outdoor paints warning that its use inside would result in peeling and could be harmful if ingested by children.

The proposal was well received and we were successful. It became clear that I was a rising star in the organization. General Battley, as was his custom with new favorites, took me to lunch at the Army-Navy Club in Washington.

We chatted amiably for a few minutes when Battley noticed I still did not have a place setting in front of me. Imperiously, he snapped his fingers for the captain of the waiters.

"Captain," he said militarily, "this is Charles Lipsen. He is my guest. He does not have tools with which to eat. I believe you'd agree, sir, it is outrageous."

His voice carried throughout the dining room and I was, to say the least, discomfited.

"General," I whispered as the captain rushed away to correct the outrage by upbraiding the waiter assigned to our table, "why didn't you just call the waiter over? He would have . . ."

"Son," he interrupted, "I want to tell you something about command—and I want you to learn. The waiter made a foolish mistake. If I had let it pass, he'd probably make the same mistake again. The only way to make certain he won't repeat it is to complain to his superior."

I nodded, but I wasn't sure I could agree. This was, after all, a restaurant and the man a waiter. It wasn't Normandy and the offender wasn't a forgetful platoon leader.

I let it pass, though, until three days later, when he summoned me to his office. I walked in and he didn't look up from the papers he was shuffling on his desk. It was a ploy I had seen military officers use a few times with their inferiors. I stood shifting from foot to foot for what seemed like minutes. But he never once looked up.

At last, he glanced up and looked at me as if I were an unexpected sight.

"Ah, Charles," he said, getting up and circling the desk to shake my hand as if this were a formal meeting. He steered me to a chair opposite his desk and pulled up one next to mine. "What I wanted to tell you," he said, "is that I've been very pleased with your work. Do you see that chair?" he asked, gesturing toward his large cushioned chair behind his desk. "If you continue to do your job well and, just as important, remain loyal to me and my directives, you'll sit in that chair one of these days."

I was silent.

"Well, Charles?" he asked. "What do you have to say to that?"

I thought a moment and decided, not for the first or last time in my life, to do the impolitic thing—but one that would make me feel good inside.

"I appreciate that, General."

"I thought you would," he said, pursing his lips at the somewhat harsh tone in my voice.

"But," I added, "I don't think I'd be interested in sitting in it."

"I'm not sure," he said, bristling, "I know what you mean."

"I'll tell you what I mean," I said, my voice hardening as I stood. "You know how you treated me just now? Like you treat everyone. Like a servant. You had me stand here at attention while you ignored me, pretending I wasn't even here. That doesn't show much respect for people. And if you don't treat people with respect, I don't see how you can expect their loyalty in return."

I headed for the door before he had a chance to answer. "I'm not your man," I said. "I'll just pick up my check and leave."

I had already noticed in working on Capitol Hill that those senators and representatives who rose to leadership positions invariably were gracious and, despite the aura of power and command that followed most of them, never imperious. It had seemed to me that General Battley was trying to imitate those in power so that by aping them he would somehow become like them. But in so doing, he had become only a caricature of those who truly possessed authority. It was clear to me that prolonged association with Battley would lead to me assuming his own poses so that I should remain his favorite. And what awaited me at the end of what I thought would be at least several years of acting like a horse's ass and losing most of my friends in Congress? Becoming executive director of an association of paint manufacturers. It hardly seemed worth the candle.

If that was lobbying, I didn't want any more of it.

Again, I was out of a job and, again, Andy Federline gave me a post until I could find something else. This time it was the National Milk Producers Federation, a natural for a Wisconsin boy like myself. Our big fight at the time was the effort to prevent manufacturers of oleomargarine from coloring their product yellow. In its natural white state, it didn't look like butter. We feared that once the color was added, people would mistake the oleo for the higher-priced spread. Eventually they lost that battle, but the job turned out to be a boon to me.

For one thing, those who had been running the organization

for some years were nearing retirement. That meant a quick promotion route for me and in 1955 I became the assistant to the general counsel, Dick Garstang. For another, Garstang was a Republican. From him, I learned early both the ease with which a Democrat could work with a Republican and, more important, the necessity of doing so if one was to be a successful lobbyist.

To be sure, I was assigned almost exclusively to Democratic members of Congress when I worked to support or oppose legislation affecting the dairy industry. But, of necessity, I called on Republicans, too.

"Listen," Garstang explained one day, "not only do we have a lot of Republicans from dairy states, but it's a question of facing reality. You can't count on people from your own party or even your regular friends to support you all the time. It's important at least to touch base with everybody, even those you don't expect to be on your side. Someday, you'll be surprised at the votes you'll pick up." Then he added: "Besides, if a congressman is on a committee dealing with a piece of legislation, he has an obligation to listen to both sides of a story before making up his mind."

I was to remember that during the remainder of my career. Not only did I win some unexpected votes for my trouble, but I also ran into some situations in which I found some members who would rather not be bothered by the facts. Knowing who they are saves one a lot of time.

An example was a recent effort of mine to see a young, bright member of Congress who had come to national attention during the televised hearings of the House Judiciary Committee considering the impeachment of Richard Nixon.

By all rights, the member should have been a personal ally of the cable TV business I was then representing. A Democrat and a liberal, the member had no perceptible ties to the networks and the motion picture industry that were opposing the expansion of the cable television business. A member of the committee considering the copyright law, the representative would have a key vote on the issue. But when I tried to make an appointment to discuss the position of the National Cable Television Association, my calls were not returned. After three tries, I asked one of the aides if there was a problem.

"No problem," I was told. "But the representative already has made a decision on the issue. There isn't any reason to discuss it further."

I knew, then, which way the decision would go.

"But," I said, "I just want to present our story."

"No need. It won't change anything."

Then, as I am wont to do from time to time, I lost my temper.

"Godammit," I blurted. "You can say there's a damn *obligation* to hear me out before a congressman makes a decision. A congressman doesn't only represent one little district. When one's on the Judiciary Committee, a congressman represents the whole country."

Whether or not my message got through, it didn't change anything. I never heard back, and I am certain my outburst means I cannot count the member among my friends in Congress. None of my tricks might have worked anyway—taking to the representative's office constituents from the cable TV business, familiarizing the member with the numbers of people in the congressional district that subscribe to cable TV, offering results of studies indicating how many more would take cable if it were offered. But I do think there was a responsibility to listen, nonetheless. The member of Congress who refuses to consider opposing points of view is not fulfilling his or her function as a lawmaker.

But there was respite for me in my first months of lobbying despite my experience with General Battley and the failure, after I left the milk lobby, to keep the anti-oleo movement successful. Relief came through the Young Democrats. I was growing to love politics. It had all the glamor and excitement of war—its strategy, its intelligence gathering, its plots to outwit the opposing force—without its concomitant bloodshed.

At about that time, in 1955, the YDs gathered in Oklahoma City for a national convention. Neil Metcalf, an Alabama state senator and a progressive (despite the times and his geographical background) selected me to co-ordinate his campaign. I liked Metcalf—but I liked even more the opportunity to run a political campaign.

It was a challenge. Many liberals in the organization could not accept the notion of electing an Alabaman as president. "He might be a liberal," a delegate from Massachusetts told me, "but unless he marries a Negro, no one will believe it."

Before the convention, I argued with delegates over the country via telephone about Metcalf's liberal voting record on civil rights proposals which had never passed his state senate. "It took more guts than you or I have for him to have voted for those things. It looks to me," I hissed at a delegate from New York City, "that you're the one who's the bigot."

By the time we got to Oklahoma City, Metcalf's opponent, David Bunn (later to become a high official in the U. S. Post Office Department) was clearly in the lead. Bunn's campaign manager, a young Californian named Phillip Burton, called me one morning to suggest we avoid any possible internal rifts and simply agree to elect Bunn by acclamation.

"You're really cute," I told Burton. "Hell, man, we haven't begun to fight."

"Okay," he laughed pleasantly. "It's your funeral."

I knew I had my work cut out with Burton as my opposite number. He was hard-working and shrewd, the kind of qualities that later led him to a seat in Congress and an important post of leadership among the Democratic members of the House of Representatives. I knew I wouldn't be able to wrestle away from him any commitments he had received from delegates. But there were still several large uncommitted delegations, most notably those from my own state of Wisconsin and from Minnesota and Michigan. If we could somehow get their votes, I thought that two or three other large northern delegations would swing behind us and we might just nose out Bunn.

I continued surveying the delegates and lobbying for Metcalf. I argued that putting a liberal Southerner at the head of our organization would encourage other liberals in the South who, until then, were afraid to buck popular opinion in their region, to take more moderate public positions and thus provide the kind of leadership that could avoid possible bloodshed.

Then the idea hit me.

"There's a way we can win," I told Metcalf one night. "But it's gonna take guts."

"What have you got in mind?" he asked cautiously.

"You take a black for your running mate."

He thought for a moment. I could see the wheels spinning in his head. Running hand-in-glove with a black for the two top offices of the Young Democrats would cause political trouble for Metcalf in Alabama. It was one thing to suggest in an all-white Alabama State Senate that everyone should be equal under the law. It was quite another to embrace a black as a political equal. And while outside the South it was then fashionable for politicians to champion the cause of equal justice for Negroes, few northern politicians had to face the reality of large black populations. It was, after all, only a year after the Supreme Court decision prohibiting racial segregation in public schools. A man named King was a minister of a black church in Montgomery, Alabama, but he was barely known outside his state and his famous bus boycott had not yet begun. In brief, the great civil rights movement that King would lead and that would arouse overpowering national sentiment for the southern Negro was, at that time, a barely fertilized embryo.

And, to top it off, my suggested choice to be Metcalf's running mate, a young black from Michigan, was a woman, to boot. Women were not strangers to politics. Both my wife and my sister were active in Democratic organizations. But, for the most part, they held offices such as party secretary or program chairman or national committeewoman. They were not presidents or vice-presidents of large political groups.

"We'd really make a little history, wouldn't we?" Metcalf said at last. "Let's do it."

I moved into action. First, I put the proposition to the Michigan delegation and especially to the woman we wanted on the ticket. She agreed promptly to the proposal.

"It's good, Chuck," she said. "I can't think of anything that would do more to help race relations right now in the country."

"That's the whole idea," I lied. The truth was that I wanted to win. Making a contribution to racial harmony was only an afterthought, if a happy one.

Then I summoned leaders of the Wisconsin and Minnesota delegations to a meeting in my room, along with representatives from the Michigan group. By 3:30 A.M., it looked as if we had the deal sealed. The one sticking point was whether the southern delegations would stay hitched to Metcalf.

"Don't worry about that," I assured. "Neil has been canvassing the delegations all night and everything looks good."

But then it happened. Metcalf called me on the room telephone. "We've got a problem," he said.

"What's happening?" I asked, trying to sound cheerful so as not to arouse any uneasiness among the others.

"Most everyone will buy the program," he said. "We'll lose Mississippi, Georgia and maybe South Carolina."

"Them too?" I lowered my voice to a whisper. "I think we can get them to stay hitched. I'll have Olin Johnston give them a call. They're his boys."

"That's good," Metcalf said. "To tell you the truth, though, it won't be good enough." He paused. "It looks like Alabama's pulling out."

"Oh, no," I said, a bit too loudly. I saw the others turn toward me. "Look, can I have a shot at them?"

"They've already sent a spokesman. He's on the way to the room now."

"Maybe it'd be better for me to do it there."

"It would," he said. "But they insist it be the other way."

As I hung up, the others looked at me expectantly.

"Well," I said, rubbing my hands together and smiling. "It looks okay. Two states are pulling out—Mississippi and Georgia. South Carolina is worried, but I'll have Senator Johnston put them back on the track. He's an old friend."

I hesitated, trying to prepare them for the big problem.

"Look, a guy's on his way up here now. From Alabama. They, uh . . . they're not too happy."

"What you're trying to say," one of the Minnesotans said laconically, "is they're planning to pull out and go for Bunn."

A groan went up. We all knew that when a state didn't back it's own favorite son, it usually proved to be the kiss of death. It was only symbolic; Alabama wouldn't have enough votes by itself to defeat us if the rest of us stayed together. But symbols are important in politics. If Alabama did not support Metcalf, other

73

southern states would be hard-pressed to do so. If Metcalf had no southern support, victory was improbable. But even if we could still pull it out, it would mean that Metcalf, as the choice of what would be seen as northern liberals in defiance of the South, would be politically impotent from then on. He needed the South to survive and have a personal political future.

Someone knocked at the door. I let in a short, broad-shouldered man with his hair slicked back and his lip curling defiantly. He had been drinking heavily.

I pointed to a chair but he refused to sit.

"Naw," he said. "What I got to say won't take but a minute. It's this. If y'all go ahead with this thing, Alabama's pullin' out lock, stock and barrel. And without us, y'all won't have a prayer."

"Don't be hasty," I said. "If we put this thing together, it'll put Alabama on the map."

"It'll put us on the map, all right. Just like Hiroshima got put on the map."

"I can talk to Frank Long and the governor," I said. "They know me and I know they'll go along." Frank Long was Metcalf's campaign manager for Alabama. And the governor was Jim Folsom. Metcalf was Folsom's floor leader in the Alabama Senate and despite Folsom's widely publicized flamboyance, he was a progressive for his time and styled himself as a Truman Democrat despite the almost irreparable rift between Truman and the Dixiecrats in 1948.

"I've already talked to 'em both," the Alabaman said. "They both good friends-a mine, too, you know. Maybe I even know 'em a little better'n you do."

"Well, what did they say?"

"They agreed with me," he said, teetering slightly from the whisky he had consumed, "that this ain't the time to have any damn niggers on the ticket."

"Now, you look here," I said, the blood rising in my face. "You don't have to talk that way. You show a little respect."

"I'm just tellin' you the way it is."

"I know damn well that neither Long nor the governor said that."

74

"Well," he allowed, "maybe they didn't say 'nigger.' Naw, they was more polite. But whether you wanna say 'nigger' or you wanna say 'Nee-ger-o,' it's all the same. We ain't havin' any of 'em on the ticket. If we do, Alabama goes against it's own man."

"Well, I guess that wraps it up," a Wisconsin delegate said.

"Wait a minute," I pleaded. "If we stay together we can still pull it out."

"No way, Chuck. The whole South'll follow Alabama. Neil can't run without his own state, much less the South."

I knew we were beaten. The whole thing had been in the palms of our hand and then it blew up when that little Alabama bastard strutted in. As much from frustration as from any sense of being offended at his manner toward Negroes, I turned on him.

"Okay, you son of a bitch," I said menacingly, putting my whole bulk directly in front of him and peering down. "You and your dirty mouth just get the hell out of my room."

He leered up at me through heavy-lidded eyes. "I better tell you, fella," he said, "that I might be a little drunk but I useta be a fighter."

"So did I," I said through my teeth, "and I've got some height and weight on you."

"Okay, okay, you guys," one of the delegates said, stepping between us. "Let's break it up. This isn't Madison Square Garden." He turned to the Alabaman. "You better get out," he said.

The little man turned, still looking me in the eye and, with as much dignity as he could muster despite the drink, he started out of the room. Then I lunged forward, grabbed him under the arms, lifted him into the hallway, and slammed the door behind him.

I slumped into the bed as the room emptied out. In a few moments, there was a tap at the door. It was Neil Metcalf. He took one look at my face and knew what had happened.

"It was that prick you sent up here," I said, my words tired despite their vehemence.

"I didn't send him," Metcalf said. "He was their choice. He's not even a delegate. But they knew you couldn't budge him. He even says he talked Folsom and Long into dropping out if we

75

went ahead with the plan." He sighed. "It was a good try, Chuck. We'll go ahead with someone else on the ticket and do the best we can." We both knew it wouldn't be enough.

"Who is that guy?" I asked. "He never even told me his name."

"He's a county judge," Metcalf said. "Used to be one of Folsom's protégés in the legislature. Believe it or not, he's considered one of the moderates down home. I know he sounded awful, Chuck. He'd been drinking quite a bit. But he figured it would kill off people like himself or me, cut us off from any political future, if we went out on a limb like running with a black. And, much as I hate to admit it, he's probably right."

"What's his name?" I asked.

"Wallace. George Wallace."

I hate to admit it, too, but the Little Judge *was* right. Some three years later, in 1958, he ran for governor of Alabama with the support of Folsom, Metcalf and other moderates against John Patterson, the state's attorney general, who accepted the support of the Ku Klux Klan.

Wallace had tried to appear less of a moderate by publicly threatening that, as a judge in Barbour County, he would place under arrest any agent of the FBI or any other federal officer who tried to inspect the voting records in the county to determine if Negroes were systematically kept from voting. Privately, however, Wallace had assured U. S. District Court Judge Frank Johnson, who had ordered the voting rolls inspected, that he would personally deliver the records to the court. Wallace explained that while the order would thus be complied with, he could maintain an attitude of defiance necessary to his chances for victory over Patterson. Johnson reluctantly agreed, wanting to avoid a head-on collision between federal and state authorities. And it is a good bet that Johnson, a moderate Republican whose first major decision as a judge was to declare unconstitutional segregation on city buses, preferred a posturer like Wallace as governor to an outspoken racist like Patterson.

The ploy didn't work, however, and Patterson defeated Wallace soundly. "Nobody'll ever out-nigger me again," Wallace later told some cronies. Along the line, Wallace also became a teetotaler and icily set about to develop what would become one of the most formidable political dynasties in the history of the South. En route to his election as governor in 1962, he supposedly destroyed his old mentor, Jim Folsom, by spreading the word that Folsom was an alcoholic (an allegation that was, if never proved, believed to be close to the truth). And his notorious "segregation forever" inaugural set the tone of racial hatred in the South for the rest of that turbulent decade.

I had told it to the judge that night in Oklahoma City. But, as with nearly all his political opponents, he had defeated me. Had it been otherwise, I thought many times over the years, history might have taken a sharply different turn.

Would the election by the YDs of a white Southerner running with a black woman have encouraged the entire South to take a stance of moderation? Or would it have led to the surfacing of men even more potentially dangerous than George Wallace?

We'll never know. But I'll always wonder.

8

KEFAUVER, KENNEDY—
AND A KONNIVER

Early in 1956, Mike Norton, a lobbyist for the National Milk Producers, walked into my office and made a brief announcement.

"You're going to work for Estes Kefauver," he said. He explained that he and Kefauver had just chatted about the senator's upcoming campaign for the Democratic presidential nomination. The Milk Producers couldn't give Kefauver much money, Norton had said, but the organization could split off one of its energetic young lawyers to work full time for Kefauver during his campaign.

I was a natural choice. Kefauver had been instrumental in luring me to Washington, even though he hadn't a job for me when I arrived. I had remained in touch with him over the previous years and, at the 1952 Democratic National Convention in Chicago, Olin Johnston had detailed me to Kefauver's political forces to assist them in their unsuccessful bid to wrest the nomination from Governor Adlai Stevenson of Illinois.

That year, 1952, I was given floor credentials and assigned to circulate among the delegations to size up whether there were any shifts or changes among those delegates pledged to any candidate, and then to report to Kefauver's campaign managers whom they might see to pick up any new votes, or where they might have to shore up crumbling support.

But there was a problem and it was called Richard Daley.

Mayor Daley of Chicago was eager to push through the nomination of Stevenson, his state's governor. Accordingly, Daley assigned a squad of local police to the convention floor for "security." The security consisted of careful checking of floor credentials to prevent one or another candidate from counterfeiting the passes so as to have an excess of his own workers circulating through the delegations in behalf of their man. The idea was reasonable enough—but Daley had no visceral dislike for rigging conventions, as long as they were rigged his way.

He provided his security force with lists of names of those people favorable to Stevenson who might be expected on the floor. Those people could enter the convention arena at will—with or without credentials. But those of us working for candidates other than Stevenson, even when we had proper floor passes, did not appear on the list and were subjected to harassing delays of up to five minutes while the guards were "checking" the authenticity of the credentials.

I was growing angrier each time I tried to get on the floor until, after one particularly long delay—which included a patdown search for weapons that I considered an appalling insult and embarrassment, I saw a modishly dressed young man standing near the podium who wore no credentials. I rushed over to Ray Jacobson, one of Kefauver's floor lieutenants.

"Do you see that guy over there in the gray suit?" I demanded. "He's got no goddam credentials. Let's get his ass kicked the hell out of here and give Daley some of his own medicine."

Jacobson looked where I was pointing.

"Let's not make a production out of it," he said. "That's Joe Kennedy's kid. He's a congressman from Massachusetts."

"I don't care if he's God Almighty," I fumed. "You need cre-

79

dentials to be on the floor. That's what Daley's goons have been screaming at us all week."

Jacobson shrugged and I headed toward Joe Kennedy's kid.

"You're not supposed to be on the floor," I challenged as I approached him.

"Oh?" he said absently. "Why not?"

"You don't have credentials, that's why not."

"Are you the sergeant-at-arms? he asked lightly.

"No. I'm just a slob working for Kefauver. They give us a hell of a time here. But you must be one of Daley's boys, right?"

He looked at me for a moment and then flashed a wide grin that lighted his face. "Not yet," he said. "But I hope to be. I like winners." Then he turned and walked away.

I hadn't even let on that I knew he was a congressman and, despite my pique, I admired him for not trying to pull rank. And I knew what he meant about winners. Politicians with ambition never amounted to much more than glorified dog-catchers if they associated with the likes of Alf Landon.

I was still smarting over the apparent Daley-inspired injustices of the convention when two uniformed guards approached me. One looked at my floor pass, checked the number and turned to the other.

"This is the one," he said.

Without further ceremony, each man grabbed me by an arm and began purposefully hustling me off the floor.

"What the hell's going on?" I blurted.

They didn't answer but simply bullied me through an exit. One then grabbed the credentials hanging from a chain around my neck and jerked them off.

For the next few moments, I was uncharacteristically speechless. A sudden wave of fear weakened my knees. I was afraid, mindlessly, that they would beat me, right there in the hallways of the convention building.

At that moment, two men bustled up brandishing note pads. One was my old friend Jack Anderson. The other was a mustachioed man whose face was almost as familiar in the country at that time as Harry Truman's. It was Drew Pearson.

"What's going on here?" Pearson asked imperiously.

"Nothing, nothing at all," one of the cops replied.

"I'm Drew Pearson," he said, flashing his credentials. "I understand Mayor Daley has been putting the muscle on anyone opposing Governor Stevenson. Is that true?"

The two guards mumbled something incoherent and walked away.

"You okay?" Anderson asked.

"I'm okay. It's lucky you guys came along. I could have sworn they were going to rubber-hose me or something."

"Well," Pearson said. "They probably wouldn't have gone that far. But we didn't want to take any chances."

"Your friend Ray Jacobson spotted us," Anderson said, "and told us to make sure you were okay."

"What the hell happened, anyway?" I asked, genuinely puzzled. "One minute I was walking along, minding my own business, and the next . . ."

"And the next you stopped and hollered at Jack Kennedy."

"That kid congressman?" I asked. "Joe Kennedy's son?"

"The very same," Anderson said.

"He must not have liked what you said to him," Pearson added. "He evidently called in some of Daley's bullyboys to see that you were removed from the floor."

It was not the last run-in I was to have with Jack Kennedy. The next one occurred in 1956, when I agreed to become one of Kefauver's lieutenants in his next campaign to become the presidential nominee.

The primaries that year had been hectic, but when we reached Chicago, where the next convention also was held, it was clear that Stevenson would again be the Democratic nominee to challenge, however vainly, Dwight Eisenhower.

Most of us in the Kefauver camp that year were listlessly resigned to certain defeat. But then Stevenson, in a desperate attempt to bolster the sagging Democratic spirits, unprecedentedly decided to throw open the party's nomination for Vice-President rather than hand-pick his own running mate.

Stevenson's ploy had its effect. For the first time in months, excitement surged through the delegations to the convention. Of a

81

sudden, there were a half-dozen serious contenders for the vice-presidential nomination, Kefauver high among them.

The others included Averell Harriman of New York, Stuart Symington of Missouri, Albert Gore (Tennessee's other senator), and a young man recently elected to the Senate, John F. Kennedy of Massachusetts.

Of all the possibilities, Kefauver had campaigned the longest and the hardest. The upstart, Jack Kennedy, would be no problem. The urbane Stevenson would prefer to balance his ticket with a Southerner (as he had with John Sparkman of Alabama in 1952) or a Midwesterner and, though he technically was staying out of the battle, he would presumably make at least that much known. The ticket could hardly be strengthened by an Easterner with a Harvard education who was a Catholic besides.

That left Symington and Gore to worry about. Of the two, Gore was our biggest headache. He was from the same state as Kefauver. But he had the advantage of being supported by the head of the Tennessee delegation, Governor Frank Clement, who had been that year's convention keynote speaker (and whose memorable denunciation of Eisenhower leading the nation down "the long, green fairway of indifference" would long be remembered). Clement despised Kefauver as a maverick. Worse, the governor, who liked to put on airs of being little more than a simple country boy, believed Kefauver was pretentious and overbearing personally. Gore, on the other hand, regularly sought the governor's advice on political matters and paid Clement at least lip service as head of the party in Tennessee.

Again, as I had in my Young Democratic efforts, I would face the problem of a candidate's own state deserting him in his pursuit of high office.

As it turned out, all the initial candidates received reasonable support in the opening ballots, but it was clear that Kefauver was moving toward certain victory. Then, without warning, southern states switched to young Kennedy. It was an amazing move. Of any section in the country, the South might have been least expected to support the candidacy of a Catholic, especially one from Massachusetts. But, as my checking quickly showed, there were at least two good reasons. First, Southerners held little affection for Kefauver, whom they viewed as a turncoat on civil rights issues. They believed the Tennessee senator had betrayed his region to gain national stature and the resulting opportunity for the party's nomination for President. Second, the 1956 Democratic nomination for Vice-President took place in an almost make-believe atmosphere. Not only was it totally out of character for a convention to be nominating a Vice-President without first having been told whom they should select, but the delegates frankly didn't give a damn. There was no way to beat Eisenhower and they knew it. Whomever they chose might be able to gain some fleeting national attention but, they reasoned, would quickly fade from the scene after the anticipated debacle in November.

The bloc of southern votes for Kennedy suddenly thrust him into contention. Then there were switches that gave his candidacy momentum while Kefauver's totals were beginning to slide. Football commentators incessantly talk about one team or the other having "momentum." That may be so much hogwash as far as football is concerned, but it's an uncontrovertible reality as far as politics goes. In 1968, Lyndon Johnson was forced to yield his presidency because of Eugene McCarthy's showing in the New Hampshire primary. Johnson won the balloting there handily. But McCarthy did much better than expected. He had the momentum, small as it was, and even from a politically insignificant state. In 1972, the same thing happened, in reverse, to Edmund Muskie. Largely because of his display of human emotion, he did not run as well as had been expected in New Hampshire. He had been the odds-on favorite; when, in relation to that, he fared poorly, he had lost his momentum and soon was out of the race.

For Kefauver, something had to be done—and quickly—to restore his momentum.

I ranged over the floor of the convention, trying desperately to develop scraps of political intelligence that would suggest how we could restore Kefauver's drive toward the nomination.

I scurried to catch up with a friend of mine in the generally unfriendly Tennessee delegation. What he told me persuaded me that Kefauver was doomed.

"We're gonna stick with Gore for a couple of ballots," the friend confided. "But then, when Gore withdraws, I'm afraid the governor has decided he'll switch to Kennedy."

"My God," I breathed. "He's *got* to go with his own senator after Gore is out of the picture."

"Where is that written?" my friend said with a bemused grin. "Clement can do anything he wants—and he wants to bury Kefauver."

I headed up the aisle, morose and defeated. Where could we pick up some new strength? I passed the Oklahoma delegation when I saw an old friend from Young Democrats.

"I think we've got good news for your man," he said.

"I need some," I answered.

"We just caucused and Mike [Senator Mike Monroney] made a helluva pitch for Estes. We agreed to switch from Gore to Estes."

"When?" I asked, my tone reflecting the intensity of my feelings.

"In a ballot or two."

"No!" I almost shouted above the din. "You've got to do it now! If you don't, Kennedy's gonna pick up some more votes and we'll be dead."

"You better talk to Mike," he said gravely.

He hustled me over to the senator. One of the points I had in my favor is that through my work with the YDs, I had been the program chairman in Washington. That meant I would invite senators and congressmen to speak not only to the local group but also to meetings which leaders from different parts of the country would attend. Members of Congress liked to be regularly exposed to the younger, developing leaders in the party so they could keep expanding their political base.

"What's up, Chuck?" he asked, and laughed. It was Monroney's private joke. One of the first times I had called on him in my capacity as a lobbyist for the milk interests, a subject not especially close to a senator from the West, I was gravely worried about our chances to defeat the oleo interests, and I looked it. "What's up, Chuck?" he asked then, and added, "You look like you're going to upchuck."

This time, I must have looked exactly the same way. "I understand you're switching to Estes," I said, hoping I wasn't violating my friend's confidence but too concerned to worry about it.

"We are," he said, his eyes veiling.

"Senator, you've got to move now. We're on the downslide and if we don't get a shot in the arm, I'm afraid we've had it."

He thought a moment and said, "I think we can do that."

"Great!" I exploded.

"But," he added quickly, "we've got to get recognition from the chair. Can you arrange it?"

I glanced to the podium, where the venerable Speaker of the House of Representatives, the crusty Sam Rayburn of Texas, stood, gavel in hand, recognizing state delegations who wanted to switch their votes. Rayburn had the authority, as convention chairman, to recognize states in whatever order he chose at this stage of the voting. Rayburn was not enamored of young Jack Kennedy. There were rumors he objected to Kennedy's youth and his Catholicism. But he despised Kefauver, as did many Southerners, both for his sometimes abrasive personality and for his independence in breaking southern ranks on the race issue. Rayburn hated most, of all things political, a lack of party discipline, even if sometimes he did not personally agree with the cause at hand.

"I'll see what I can do," I said.

I had no time to check with Kefauver himself, so I summoned several of our floor lieutenants together and told them my plan. We all hustled to the podium, where three or four men boosted me up on their shoulders so that Rayburn could see me.

Rayburn, of course, knew who I was though he did not know me well, a situation that would change dramatically in later years. At that time, though, he knew I was one of Kefauver's key men at the convention.

The noise and confusion in the hall grew in direct proportion to the growing excitement over the pitched battle between old pro Kefauver and young upstart Kennedy.

Gore had announced he was pulling out of the race, and he personally endorsed Kefauver. But Clement was pulling the strings in the Tennessee delegation. And if Tennessee were formally recognized after Gore's dramatic announcement, I knew it would be all over for us. Clement would just as dramatically go for Kennedy. By now, however, the Speaker was spending much of his time rapping his gavel and calling the convention to a semblance of order. He looked like King Canute trying to turn back the waves of the sea.

I started shouting and waving my arms frantically like a deck officer on an aircraft carrier warning off a landing plane.

"Tennessee!" I screamed. "Tennessee! Call Tennessee! They're going Kefauver! Tennessee!"

I saw him glancing down at me, but his impassive face neither showed if he heard me—nor if he wanted to. But I kept on.

"Not Oklahoma!" I shouted even louder than before, wagging my head from side to side. "Not Oklahoma! They're going Kennedy! Not Oklahoma! Call Tennessee! Tennessee is Kefauver!"

I kept it up for what seemed like minutes. Still, despite the spectacle I was creating, I couldn't tell if Rayburn even heard me.

At last, over the rapping of his gavel, a sound magnified by the loudspeaker system, Rayburn began to chant the name of a state which he was recognizing.

"Oklahoma," he intoned. "Does Oklahoma desire recognition?"

I almost collapsed from my efforts and nearly fell to the floor from the shoulders that had been holding me in the air. It had worked. Or, perhaps in spite of me, Rayburn had called Oklahoma anyway. Basing my tactics on the belief that Rayburn would do anything to avoid putting Kefauver over the top, even to the point of accepting a Kennedy candidacy, I tried a bit of reverse psychology. In urging him to recognize Tennessee, shouting it was ready to shift to Kefauver (a totally plausible scenario, even to a political war-horse like Rayburn), and screaming that it was necessary to avoid calling on Oklahoma, which, I had bellowed, was ready to go for Kennedy, I was hoping the Speaker would do exactly the opposite. He did. And when the spokesman for Oklahoma, finally getting a reasonable amount of attention from the assembled delegates, spoke into his microphone, I knew we had won:

"Mr. Chairman," he said, "Oklahoma desires to change its vote from Senator Gore, since he released us." The vote, he declared, now was being cast for the next Vice-President of the United States, the Honorable Estes Kefauver!

Pandemonium broke out among Kefauver factions. The Speaker rapped his gavel and looked chagrined. By now, I was standing to one side of the podium, lost in a crowd of hats and banners. I thought I saw Rayburn scowling and scanning the delegates assembled on the floor for that fellow who had foxed him. I don't think he saw me. And if he remembered it had been I who pulled the trick on him—a trick which at that point turned the tide and assured Kefauver's nomination (his "abomination," one of the Tennessee delegates called it later)—he never let on to me.

It was just as well. I felt somewhat badly for months over what I had done. It had been a fantastic coup, one which Kefauver himself likened to wartime intelligence victories by the British which turned the Allied tide against the Germans at El Alamein. But starting the next day, after the flush of victory had left me, I had misgivings. I had been a fraud. I had lied. Not to just anyone, mind you, but to the powerful and revered Speaker Sam Rayburn. It became for me a hollow victory of the spirit.

I have since rationalized by persuading myself that I had a hand in helping make John Kennedy President of the United States four years later. There is no question in my mind that had he been the Democratic vice-presidential candidate in the electoral debacle that followed in November of 1956, he would not have had a prayer of winning the presidential nomination four years later. The defeat itself would have been overwhelming. After the Cox-Roosevelt ticket went down in flames in 1920, it took FDR another dozen years to recover enough to win his own presidential nomination. But Kennedy was also a Catholic, and it seems clear that factor would have been cited again and again as the reason the Democrats lost so badly in 1956.

As it turned out, Kefauver had won a Pyrrhic victory while Kennedy, in defeat, had demonstrated that a young Eastern Catholic could command support even from his party's conservative southern wing.

But Kefauver was nonetheless elated, and I began to crisscross America in search of votes that would never come.

9

IF IT'S TUESDAY,
IT MUST BE PITTSBURGH

An advance man for Estes Kefauver in 1956 had to be a combination of Marco Polo, the Great Kreskin and one of Colonel Hall's Raiders.

In less than three months, I logged 80,000 miles crisscrossing the country, much of it in borrowed cars along back roads trying to find towns like Ponca City, Oklahoma. I had to file in my memory the names of Democratic leaders and workers—not to mention those of their wives plus their businesses and problems —from nearly every city and county in about half the continental United States. And I had to move around with a budget so tight that I survived on a basic diet of hamburgers and ice cream cones and frequently had to spend the night curled up in the back seat of a car.

If time permitted, an advance man would get to a city for a major rally a week ahead of the candidate. When I arrived, say, at Oklahoma City, I would begin by getting in touch with both the state and local Democratic leaders. By that time, these people had appointed a couple of others as chairmen of the planned rally and, presumably, some tentative arrangements had been made.

As usual, the arrangements called for the candidate to shake hands with about two-thirds of the city's population. There would be a seven-thirty businessmen's breakfast, a tour of downtown and shopping centers, a TV taping for a local talk show, a noon news conference, a ladies' luncheon, a session in a hotel room with local political leaders, a visit to local campaign headquarters, a media event suitable for photos (such as a visit to a poor neighborhood or a nearby Indian village to demonstrate the candidate's concern for the have-nots), a private cocktail party for major contributors, the big rally or fund-raising dinner, the after-rally handshaking, holding private court in the candidate's hotel room for those two or three individuals who might be induced to double their contributions, and a day's-end briefing by staff members about the next day's activities before the candidate retired at 3 A.M.

It was my job and that of every candidate's advance man to inspect each and every site selected for each event, make certain there was proper sound equipment available for each address, ascertain that the halls in which Kefauver would appear had sufficient electrical power to handle TV lights, notify all local media of the candidate's plans, go over seating plans and who would be coming through receiving lines to meet the senator, arrange to borrow a Cadillac with a driver for Kefauver's arrival, make sure signs of support were prepared, see to it that local labor unions and friendly employers (including whatever Democratic government offices there were) got their workers to the airport to wave those signs upon the candidate's arrival (and thus provide good film and photo possibilities), and even try to get the school board to recess school for a few minutes so the kids could line the streets along the route Kefauver would take from the airport to his hotel.

I would come close to filling a legal-sized yellow pad with notes. The requirement to inspect the places in which Kefauver would speak was not prompted by security, a consideration barely flicked at in those days preceding politics by assassination. Rather, it was to gauge their size in relation to the crowd expected. I always made sure we had a hall just a little too small to accommodate the guests. An "overflow" crowd always gave a psychological boost to campaign workers and supporters (it gave them the feeling they were part of a strong, enthusiastic team) and it almost guaranteed a positive impact on the press (who frequently would write that Kefauver spoke in a room "jammed with supporters").

To assure the proper sound and wiring at the least possible cost, I would usually get the local electricians' union to donate the time of some of its members.

The most time-consuming task involved finding out the names and vital details of all the people the senator was likely to meet during his trip. It was important not only to find out about the local fat cats, but about every last precinct worker as well. When one of the hoi polloi spent twenty-five dollars to attend a function featuring Estes Kefauver, especially with the grim Democratic national prospects of 1956, you could bet one of two things: either the guy was forced to go by a boss who otherwise might have found reason to lay him off, or he was a gung-ho party man. In either event, it was necessary to make the poor slob feel important so he would neither resent paying out his hard-earned cash nor lose his enthusiasm for putting in hours of time after his regular workday on behalf of the candidate.

I would make a stack of three-by-five cards on which I would list the names of people Kefauver would meet. I separated the stacks into the different events that had been scheduled; if the same person would be at more than one event, I would make a card for him for each function.

On each card, I would note the man's name, his wife's name, the number of his kids (and, if possible, their names and ages as well and if any were in college or were outstanding athletes), the man's occupation, what he had done for us in the campaign, how much money he had contributed (or how much he might contribute if the senator blew some smoke in his direction), and whether he had any personal problems with which the senator could sympathize.

Then I would assign a number to each of the cards. Except for the VIPs, who would lead any group into a reception to shake Kefauver's hand or who would share the dais with him, I assigned the numbers arbitrarily. The numbers were then transferred by local volunteer staff workers to name cards. As people snaked through a reception line, I would position myself about three persons ahead of Kefauver. While the person was shaking hands with, say, the state chairman and still had the mayor and possibly one of the state's senator's to go before reaching the candidate, I would note the number on his name card, shuffle through my stack to find his three-by-five, slip down the line to Kefauver, who would turn to me, glance at the card and digest as much of it as he could in the few seconds before that person would extend his hand.

"Senator," I would then say, "you remember Jack Smith, don't you?"

Then I would glance at the next person in line while Kefauver would say:

"Jack it's good to see you again. How's your wife, Minnie? Is her leg on the mend? Too bad she couldn't be here tonight. And that cow of yours, the one whose teats dried up; has she started giving again?"

Just as Jack would move off, I would move in again with the next card. And so it went until Kefauver gained the reputation of having a phenomenal memory for names and faces.

Sometimes, though, even the best laid plans of advance men go haywire. After Kefauver's long day in Oklahoma City, a bull roast was planned for Ponca City. I had commuted between Oklahoma City and Ponca City during the week, seeing to details at both. But except for arranging a caravan for the press to follow Kefauver to Ponca City and preparing the all-important list of names of people who would go through the receiving line at the bull roast, I concentrated on the fuller Oklahoma City schedule.

So when one of the workers for the Ponca City event came up with an idea for pictures at Ponca City, I listened with only one ear.

"There's this circus in town," he said excitedly, "and I think I

91

can get them to come over and have like a little parade of animals and stuff."

"Sounds good," I mumbled as I continued poring over the list of names of the people who planned to attend the roast.

"It'd make great pictures and maybe the senator could even get on and ride something," he said.

"Yeah, sure," I said absently.

I got to Ponca City early on the morning of the roast, met with local leaders and then grabbed a nap in my car in front of a seedy motel which not only didn't appeal to me but which I couldn't afford on my budget anyway. At about 11 A.M., I drove to the home of the chairman of the event. He told me I had a call from Oklahoma City.

"What's up?" I asked Kefauver's traveling campaign co-ordinator when I got through.

"The senator will be late, Chuck, maybe by an hour or so. The locals ran in some people this morning they think will give big if they had a personal meeting with the boss. I figured at this stage, it couldn't hurt to try."

"Okay," I sighed. "I'll try to keep things buzzing till he gets here."

When we got to the meadow where the rally was being staged, people were beginning to stream in. Besides the roast, booths had been set up to provide some fund-raising carnival games like horseshoe pitching and dart throwing.

But as the lea came into full view, I gasped.

"What's wrong?" my companion asked.

"What the hell is going on with those things here?"

I pointed dumbly at three huge elephants across the meadow.

"Oh, those are from the local circus we told you about. We figured maybe the senator would get up on one. It'd make a great picture."

"Jesus Christ," I sputtered, "I can't put Kefauver on one of those goddamn things. He'll get killed!"

"No, he won't. They're like big pet dogs. And the people'd get a big kick out of it. Good publicity for the circus people, too. They're doing it for free."

We drove toward the beasts while I wondered what the hell

Kefauver would say when I told him he was supposed to ride an elephant. At the very least, the man should have had some prior knowledge he would become a circus performer for the afternoon.

By the time I got out of the car and approached the trainer, the elephants had drawn a sizable crowd. I thought to myself they would become a bigger attraction than Kefauver, in popularity as well as size.

"You sure there's no danger?" I asked the trainer.

"None at all," he assured me. "They're tame and perfectly trained."

But house-trained they weren't. As we stood there, there was a whoosh of sound. One of the elephants had begun to urinate.

I had never seen an elephant urinate before and I suppose I never will again. It was like a water spout had descended from a storm cloud over the sea. Instinctively, we all darted away. But, for some, it was too late. The enormous force and amount of the animal's discharge splattered over most of us and many of the people crowded around. There were squeals of dismay. Worse, a small tidal wave formed beneath the elephant and started spilling toward us down the gradual slope leading to the pit where huge sides of beef were being turned by a spit over the open roasting fires. I was nearly up to my ankles in the stuff when I leaped to safety.

"Oh, Jesus, Chuck, I'm sorry," our host puled. "Can I do anything?"

I looked down as I tried to shake the excess moisture from my trouser cuffs. "You got an extra pair of socks in your pocket?" I asked facetiously.

I decided, however, that when Kefauver arrived the elephants would be gone. It was one thing for a candidate to put on a funny hat or even to ride an elephant for a publicity picture. It was another thing for the possible next Vice-President of the United States to get peed on.

"Okay," I said when I got the trainer and the event chairman together, "here's what we do. Kefauver's running about an hour late. So you give the kiddies some free rides for a while. But by one o'clock, I want these things back in their trucks and the hell

93

out of here. The circus'll get plenty of local exposure and we won't risk any, er, accidents when the senator gets here."

They reluctantly agreed, even after the trainer assured me that elephants don't urinate more than once a day. "Yeah," I said, "but there's two more elephants to go. They're gone by one o'clock or they go right now."

It was a relief from both the exhausting schedule that Kefauver maintained as well as a pleasant change of scenery when I was reassigned soon thereafter to perform one advancing chore for Governor Stevenson, whose own staff had been depleted by a minor flu epidemic.

Stevenson was to make a major speech in Pittsburgh and I was chosen to set up the arrangements. It was, compared to my chores for Kefauver, an easy assignment. Pittsburgh was Democratic country and the party organization was a large, tightly disciplined corps set up by David Lawrence, who, at various times, had been mayor and later governor of Pennsylvania. They were pros and there was little that required change or even double-checking.

For most of the four days I was there, I was free to rest in a fancy hotel room (at least the presidential candidate had a reasonably good budget and the local party never lacked for money) and quaff a few beers with local leaders in politics and in the labor movement.

Stevenson arrived a few hours before his evening appearance. He was resting in his room, I was told by one of his staffers, and would see me before a small, private cocktail party preceding his speech so he could be briefed on the evening's arrangements.

When I got to Stevenson's room, a man let me in who, when I introduced myself, simply nodded, limply took my hand and proceeded to wander aimlessly about the room without telling me his name or saying another word.

Then Stevenson, that dapper, punctilious man who had gotten more publicity from a hole in his shoe than from all his erudite and witty criticisms of American government under Eisenhower, walked into the living room with a towel draped around his ever so slightly paunchy middle. It took me a moment before I recognized him.

"Hi, Governor." I smiled. "I'm Chuck Lipsen from Senator Kefauver's staff. I filled in for some of your own people to advance this trip."

He looked at me, his eyes slightly glazed. Despite having just walked out of a shower with rivulets of water dripping down the sides of his face, he looked pale and drawn.

He glanced toward the other man, who, at that moment, let himself out the door of the suite.

"Who was that?" Stevenson asked.

"I don't know." I shrugged. "He didn't tell me his name." I was beginning to think I had stumbled into a rehearsal for a Noel Coward drawing room comedy.

"No matter," he sighed. Then he peered at me, seemingly trying to focus his eyes. "Where are we? What day is it?"

The man was clearly exhausted from the pace and strain of the campaign, one he knew he had no chance of winning even before he accepted the nomination.

"It's Pittsburgh, Governor," I said. "And it's Tuesday."

"Of course," he said, smiling wanly and plopping down, still damp, into an easy chair.

I figured I had better do some talking. Most men and women who are physically and emotionally drained want and need silence. But this man wasn't most people. He was a presidential candidate who had a cocktail party coming up shortly followed by a major speech which would be widely covered by the press. He had to snap out of his funk—and fast.

"Everytime I come to this town," I blurted, "I always think of that old story about the two Jesuits in New York who want to take a train to Pittsburgh. One of them, a young priest, goes to the ticket window to make the purchase when he sees nearby a simply gorgeous woman with a huge bust.

"When his turn comes, he's still glancing at the woman when the clerk says, 'What can I do for you, Father?' With his mind only half on what he's saying, the Jesuit replies: 'I'd like two pickets to Tittsburgh.'"

Stevenson chortled.

"Well," I continued, "he's very embarrassed and before he makes the purchase, he scoots back to his companion, an older, more experienced man. The young priest tells him what happened and the older man laughs. 'Don't think a thing about it, my boy,' he says. 'When you've been around as long as I have, things like beautiful women won't distract you. Here, let me have the money and I'll take care of the tickets.'

"So the older priest goes to the ticket counter and, sure enough, he sees this gorgeous blonde with the enormous bust. When his turn comes, he can't help but occasionally glancing in her direction, too. But with great will, he concentrates on his task.

" 'What can I do for you, Father?' the clerk asked.

" 'I'd like two tickets to Pittsburgh,' the priest said very carefully. Then, still looking back at the blonde, he added: 'And please let me have my change in nipples and dimes.' "

Stevenson threw back his head and roared. His whole body seemed to relax and a little color came into his cheeks. He bounced up then, told me to fix a drink for both of us, and he retired to his bedroom to dress.

To this day, though, I remember the almost gaunt look on his face when I entered his hotel suite that night. I wonder if Americans derive some sort of sadistic pleasure in having erected an electoral system that guarantees its candidates for highest office will be, at the least, mentally scrambled by the end of a political campaign.

And campaigns get longer and longer each quadrennium. By the middle of 1975, fully a year and a half before the 1976 general election, six Democrats and two Republicans were actively traveling the country to start developing their presidential campaign organizations. The number of presidential primaries had proliferated to such an extent that the newsmagazines ran charts so voters could follow them like using a scorecard at a baseball game.

Nearly every candidate, wearied by the length of the campaign and frightened by the shifting polls, had the time to take at least two positions on most major issues—but none had the time because of constant travel and handshaking and speechmaking and being interviewed to think through carefully a single cogent position on any problem. The resultant sloganeering made TV commercials, by comparison, seem almost Shakespearean in their lucidity.

Someday we may have the good sense to conduct a national primary in, say, September and limit the nominees to about two months of campaigning before the election. It might be less exciting than the current system for the professional politicians. But it would save candidates from damaged psyches and the people from damaged eardrums.

10

THE ABC OF LOBBYING

Losers weepers. That's the story of a major political campaign. I had been "on loan" to Kefauver from the National Milk Producers. That was good. It meant I retained most of my salary plus about $200 a week from Kefauver.

But at the end of the campaign, I couldn't return to my old job. I was too closely associated with Kefauver and, more importantly, with a losing campaign. A disastrously losing campaign.

But politics also requires taking care of those who toiled in your vineyard, even through a drought. When Richard Nixon was defeated by Pat Brown for governor of California in 1962, he raged and stomped in front of the media, asserting, with his typical paranoia, that the press wouldn't have Nixon to kick around any more. (It did, of course, much to Nixon's later regret.) But he nonetheless took time out to write a note to his top campaign workers thanking them for their labors and telling them to get in touch with Los Angeles lawyer Herb Kalmbach, who would help each one to find employment. (Kalmbach, a decent chap who later served time for confessing to being one of Nixon's bagmen in the Watergate scandals, did very well, including helping Bob Haldeman land a job with the J. Walter Thompson Co. Even during the early Watergate disclosures, when White House aide Dwight Chapin was forced to resign because he had been linked with the Nixon dirty tricks campaign, Kalmbach got Chapin a posh job with United Airlines, then one of Kalmbach's clients.)

So it was with me and Estes Kefauver. In my case, the easiest thing for him was to put me on the Senate payroll so the people could pay my salary for a while until I could land a job.

And that came through Kefauver as well. He introduced me to James Suffridge, a Tennessee Republican who had somehow gotten into organized labor. He was president of the fledgling Retail Clerks International Association of AFL-CIO and an old friend of Kefauver's in a state where, at that time, Republicans were rarely seen and never heard.

Suffridge wanted a legislative director; that is, he wanted somebody to put together the union's first lobbying program. Until then it had none for its nearly 400,000 members.

The reason was that the Retail Clerks was a white-collar union. Its members were employees in food chains, discount stores and specialty shops who wore white shirts to work and did not consider themselves in the same league with plumbers, printers or steelworkers. And most of the men and women who were eligible for union membership either didn't want any part of us or changed jobs so fast they didn't have time to consider us.

Suffridge reasoned that if we could push through a minimum wage bill that included retail workers we would have a heavy sales point when we continued trying to recruit new members.

When I sat down to plan a campaign, I realized there were two things for me to do simultaneously. The first was to raise political money from union members or others which could then be funneled into the next year's congressional campaigns. I wanted to be able to support candidates who would support the notion that retail clerks should have a minimum wage. But the incumbent members of Congress had to be wooed right away to start them thinking about proposing and supporting such a bill.

99

The two things fed one another: if we could show our members that congressmen were getting behind such a bill, they would be more willing to give their money to help get friendly members re-elected and hostile members unelected. At the same time, if we could show congressmen that we had money with which to support or oppose them next time around at the polls, they would be more inclined to help us and less inclined to oppose us.

For a legislative director (another euphemism for lobbyist) with no assistants, it meant a lot of work in a minimum amount of time.

I started by creating something I called the ABC—the Active Ballot Club—as the Retail Clerks' political action group. In so doing, though, I sat down with Suffridge to clear one thing that had troubled me during my short life as a lobbyist.

What some other major lobbies were doing, I had noticed, was dividing their political action fund-raisers and fund-dispensers from their people who called on Congress to push for their pet projects.

The AFL-CIO, for example, had one set of people running its powerful COPE organization, through which it raised and dispensed to politicians millions of dollars, and another set of people, headed by Andy Biemiller, running its lobbying department.

This made no sense to me. When I went up to Capitol Hill to talk to a congressman about supporting a minimum wage bill, for example, I wanted that man to know I was the same fellow who gave him $5,000 or so for his campaign—or might do so if he was on our side.

Suffridge agreed with that. And, just as important, he agreed that we should follow the Samuel Gompers philosophy that labor, when involved in politics, should reward its friends and defeat its enemies. This notion became my byword in politics. It was later refined by Jack Kennedy, who used to say that when you were crossed politically, "You don't get mad. You get even."

But rewarding one's friends always meant to me that a "friend" is a politician who helps you when you need help, whether he is a Democrat or Republican, a liberal or conservative, or even a man considered 90 per cent hostile to your

100

cause. Some of the best friends labor ever had were men who rarely voted on its side because, to have done so, would have spelled certain political defeat. But they were men who voted for labor when it desperately needed one more vote, perhaps at the committee level rather than in a later floor vote. In return, I would see to it they received labor support and money, though sometimes I made certain the money was carefully disguised (in the days before complete reporting of contributions became the law) so no one would find out the candidate was supported by organized labor.

That theory became the basis for a running feud over the next dozen or so years with Biemiller, one of the best-known labor lobbyists of the century.

Few could compare with Biemiller in mobilizing labor's friends in the country and in the Congress to unify behind a major union effort. But Biemiller had two blind spots. He was reluctant to "waste time," as he called it, by allowing his lobbyists to spend much effort presenting labor's case to those senators and representatives generally considered anti-labor. And even when such a member broke ranks to vote on our side on an important bill, he still opposed the idea of helping re-elect him against a more liberal and presumably stauncher supporter of the labor movement.

To be sure, his philosophy was clearly purer than my own. But, in the long run, mine won more battles in the halls of Congress if fewer on the editorial pages.

For one thing, most congressmen who vote the straight labor line would do so whether they got a sales job from us or not. Their constituencies were invariably loaded with working men and women who usually voted for them on the strength of their performance on bills that would increase their wages or social security benefits.

Those same workers also guaranteed the candidate a large pool of volunteer help in their campaigns. And if the candidate was being seriously challenged in a particular election he knew he could count on significant monetary infusions from the unions.

So while it certainly helped to make sure that such members

of Congress used whatever influence they could muster on behalf of major labor proposals, their votes could be counted on in any event.

But most senators and many conservative congressmen cannot afford to ignore consistently the needs and political positions of organized labor. To do so would mean ignoring and writing off what is, in many cases, a significant voting bloc that, if mobilized against a candidate, likely could defeat him when other circumstances make his incumbency shaky.

So it is that a Republican senator like Richard Schweiker of Pennsylvania can be counted on about 80 per cent of the time to give us some help, either with a meaningful committee vote, a floor vote or an abstention that will at least reduce by one the number of votes against us.

Retired Senator Margaret Chase Smith of Maine would invariably vote on labor's side, although in her case she never would accept money from us (or from practically anyone else, for that matter).

In 1970, Lloyd Bentsen, a wealthy businessman and one-time congressman, defeated in the Democratic primary Texas Senator Ralph Yarborough, who, besides Olin Johnston, had been organized labor's best friend in the South. A friend of Lyndon Johnson, Bentsen was a high-powered businessman against whom we had poured hundreds of thousands of dollars in money and manpower on Yarborough's behalf. (In the general election, Bentsen went on to defeat George Bush, later the country's top intelligence official.)

We were naturally crestfallen at losing a friend like Ralph Yarborough. We were even more chagrined that he was being replaced by a man who would clearly be a silk-stockinged anti-labor force in the Senate.

One day, Lloyd Hackler, a Texan who had been an assistant to President Johnson, suggested he take me to meet the new junior senator from Texas.

Bentsen, a rangy, handsome man, was courtly and friendly as he invited me to take a chair opposite his desk.

"I understand you supported my opponent," he said easily after a few minutes of chatting.

"Yes, sir," I said. And then, knowing he damn well knew the

extent to which we had supported Yarborough, I decided that being direct with him would be the best policy. So I added: "And, I might say, we supported him with lots of money."

"I'd have little respect for you if you hadn't," he responded. "But I'm in this chair now. So what's your problem?"

"Rule Twenty-two," I answered promptly, referring to our efforts to modify the Senate rule that allowed unlimited debate on any issue unless two-thirds of the senators voted to limit or close it.

"I'm with you on that," he answered promptly. "What else?" He had caught me off guard. I had expected to present a hatful of arguments why one of the Senate's oldest traditions—one which had been particularly kind to Southerners—should be changed. But instead I had to search my mind quickly to find another issue on which he might possibly consider supporting us.

"Well, there's minimum wage," I said. "We're trying to . . ."

"I know what you're trying to do," he said, nodding. "I approve. What else?"

This time I couldn't think of a thing. I was simply too surprised. I had been outflanked and I think he knew it.

"Am I hearing you right?" was all I could manage.

"You are," he said.

From that day, I thought that Lloyd Bentsen, if the stars were right, would make a superb candidate for President. With his looks, his charm, his ability to make intelligent decisions in a minimum amount of time, his impatience with dogma, and his constructive conservatism, I thought he would be able to reach large segments of the voters. That he was, in fact, among the first presidential contenders forced to drop out of the 1976 campaign against some demonstrably less capable and articulate opponents speaks poorly for both the American electorate and the system by which Presidents are chosen.

Nonetheless, in finding that the new Texas senator was, in fact, a potentially strong ally of labor, I had scored a lobbying coup that I was determined to milk to its limit. So instead of calling Biemiller or others with the good news, I waited until the next meeting at AFL-CIO headquarters of the entire corps of labor lobbyists.

As usual, Biemiller went down a list of senators to determine, through intelligence from our combined efforts, how they might be expected to vote on some of our key legislative efforts in the forthcoming session of Congress. He started with Rule Twenty-two. When he came to Bentsen, he glanced around the table. Several of the men shook their heads negatively and Biemiller started to mark him down as a "no" vote.

Just as his pencil touched the tally sheet before him, I spoke up.

"Bentsen's okay on Rule Twenty-two," I said almost offhandedly.

"What?" Biemiller asked as if he hadn't heard.

"Bentsen's with us on Rule Twenty-two," I repeated.

Biemiller stared down the table at me. "Are you sure?" he asked disbelievingly.

"I'm sure. And I'm sure he's with us on minimum wage, too."

That brought a buzz from the rest of the men and women around the table. Biemiller glared at me. He knew I had sprung the news on him in this manner to make the greatest possible impression on the other lobbyists. It was a point for my side in our running battle over which congressmen to court and, more importantly, which to spend labor's political money on when it came to election time.

But he was too smart—and too gentlemanly—to challenge in front of the others what I knew he believed to be questionable information. Many in the group were newer at the game than either of us. At the least, he did not want to discourage dissent by openly embarrassing me.

When the meeting was over, however, he collared me before I reached the door.

"Lipsen, there was no excuse for that," he said.

"I suppose I should have told you sooner," I admitted. "I wanted to impress you and everyone else with the idea we ought not to write off a lot of guys that we don't spend enough time or money on."

"That's not what I'm talking about," he said. "It's one thing for us to have a disagreement over policy and tactics. It's another when you come in here with bullshit to make a point."

"It's not bullshit," I said.

"Oh, come on, Chuck. There's no excuse for you acting like a jerk. Bentsen's no good and you loused up your credibility with me and everyone else here by pretending he is."

"He's a senator," I said, drawing myself up. "He gave me his word and I believe him."

"We'll see," Biemiller said.

And we did. Six months later, the leaders of the AFL-CIO from Texas came to Washington and threw a party in Lloyd Bentsen's honor at the Sheraton-Carlton Hotel.

"Six months ago," Bentsen said in answering the toasts made in his honor by his home state's labor leaders, "if anybody had told me that organized labor would have a function for me I'd have said he was out of his mind. But Chuck Lipsen came to see me and took the time to explain your positions on a number of matters of interest to labor. I can't say I agreed with him all the time. And I can't say in the years ahead I'll agree with him or with you most of the time. But I have agreed with you and expect to again at least some of the time."

Bentsen was being inordinately kind to me. The truth is I rarely had to explain anything to him. Just as on that first encounter, I simply took the time to call on him. Invariably, he knew ahead of time, through his own study of the issue and its political impact on him and his constituency, what he was going to do. I suspect he might have voted exactly the same way even if I had not shown an interest in him and his vote. But by overtly showing his interest in organized labor, he was assuring himself of some labor support and money in future campaigns.

In another instance, Representative William Ayres of Ohio was a man who had a large laboring segment in his congressional district but who generally voted the Republican line against labor measures. Time and again we had spent money to defeat him, always without success. But I continued to spend time chatting with him and bending elbows with him at a pub or two.

In 1960, Ayres faced the toughest re-election campaign of his career to that time. His problem was that the previous year, Ayres had been the brains behind the Landrum-Griffin Act, the bill designed to bring careful scrutiny of labor involvement in politics. The genesis of the bill had been the growing national antipathy to Jimmy Hoffa's Teamsters Union—its size, its strength, its alleged involvement with organized crime, and its political impact. Hoffa was no friend of the rest of the national labor movement. But labor's enemies were using Hoffa's unpopularity to get at all of us.

Ayres was from Akron, an area with a large labor constituency. But it was not big enough to beat him unless it was fully mobilized to turn out its entire potential vote plus a reasonable number of independents and fence-sitters who might not be enamored of him for other reasons. This seemed to be the year in which he could be knocked off.

He had tried to disguise his efforts for Landrum-Griffin to minimize the antagonism he knew his support of it would arouse in his district. To start with, the Eisenhower administration (which conceived the bill) tried to enlist him as its chief Republican sponsor. Democrat Phil Landrum of Georgia already had agreed to sponsor the bill as chairman of the House committee that would conduct hearings. But among the Republicans on the committee was a drunk and one so Neanderthal in his politics that most Republicans would be hesitant to support a bill with his name on it. Among the remaining Republicans, Ayres was chosen to lead the charge. A brilliant conservative legislator, he was considered by the White House the ideal Republican to lead his party's troops on the anti-Hoffa measure. Ayres begged off; he would help behind the scenes, he said, but he could not afford to be out front because of the make-up of his district. So he vetoed the idea of a Landrum-Ayres bill.

It was Ayres who suggested that Robert Griffin, then a second-term congressman from Michigan, carry the ball for the GOP. And it was Ayres who spearheaded the organized publicity campaign in favor of the bill and who took charge of generating constituent mail from voters and leaders over the country in support of the proposal.

But even though he tried to maintain a second-echelon role, those of us in labor made sure that voters in his district were aware of his key function on behalf of the bill.

That year, I was assigned to his district, among others, to help his opponent try to unseat him. On my first trip to the district, I met John Mihaly, the Democrat challenging the vulnerable Bill Ayres. Other than having false teeth which he continually picked with a matchbook, a speaking style that somehow excluded nouns and verbs from most of his sentences, and the uncanny knack of putting an audience to sleep within five minutes, the good-hearted Mihaly was an ideal candidate. I took one look at him and reported to labor leaders there was no need wasting any money on him.

For a time, I wondered how Ayres could have been so lucky as to draw as an opponent a man so completely incapable of defeating a horse's ass, much less a shrewd and capable incumbent like Ayres. I should have known better.

For one thing, I knew that Ayres had been behind the clever campaign to turn support of the Landrum-Griffin bill from a liability to an asset. His break had come when Jimmy Hoffa organized a national campaign to defeat fifty-four congressmen, including Ayres, who had both supported Landrum-Griffin and who came from districts in which they had been elected by reasonably close margins—the so-called "swing" districts.

Ayres created something he called The Committee to Help Re-elect Hoffa-Threatened Congressmen. It was hardly a catchy name and didn't lend itself to a handy acronym. But it said precisely what Ayres wanted it to say. Through organizations like the Chamber of Commerce and the National Association of Manufacturers (staunch supporters of Landrum-Griffin) he created a successful letter-writing and fund-raising campaign capitalizing on Hoffa's tainted name with the result all fifty-four congressmen were re-elected in 1960.

But, as I later learned, Ayres had done more to insure his success. While he had no primary election opposition, he decided to involve himself secretly in the Democratic primary. Surveying the field of candidates, one of whom would oppose him in November, he decided that Mihaly would be the easiest man for him to beat. Through intermediaries, Ayres funneled $5,000 of his own campaign money to Mihaly. On primary day, Ayres supporters dressed in working clothes and, in areas where Mihaly was known to have support, volunteered to shuttle people to the polls to make sure they would vote. The device worked and Mihaly narrowly won the primary.

In the general election, there was no contest. Ayres won handily in a year that he should have been defeated. But he was nobody's fool. Fearing that labor sentiment against him would continue to grow and that he would not always be able to arrange for a John Mihaly to run against him, Ayres returned to Washington with a plan to make a pro-labor splash. The opportunity came during the debate on that year's minimum wage bill. He conspicuously introduced what came to be known as the Kitchen-Ayres amendment, which supported key aspects of a minimum wage bill that he believed could pass the Congress. Later, he threw in with the final bill that had gotten support at the committee level.

For that, I saw to it that despite his reputation, Ayres received labor money from then on. Once I knew he needed to walk a fine line between standard conservatism and labor demands, I realized that on key issues he would be one of the strongest allies labor could have. The reason was that when Ayres supported a labor proposal, most Republicans in the House would go along with him. As a ranking Republican on the House Education and Labor Committee, his colleagues assumed correctly that Ayres was expert on labor matters. And they knew he was a conservative who would hardly go off the deep end for some cockamamie liberal spendthrift scheme.

It was that kind of ally I wanted to develop when I started building up the Active Ballot Club for the Retail Clerks International Association.

I traveled the nation for the ABC starting with a fund totaling three dollars which I donated as the first membership. I arranged picnics in the Midwest, an outing to Disneyland in California, raffles in the Northwest, bingo games in the East, all designed to raise money. In six months, we had a half-million dollars and I was ready to turn to Congress.

I started with the senators and representatives who were members of the committees which handled labor legislation. I would call on each, introducing myself and introducing them to the ABC, which I informed them, as subtly as possible, would be active in congressional campaigns. Then I would see those staff members who worked on labor issues for those same congressmen. The next step was to meet and befriend the leadership of both houses of Congress. That included men like Senator Lyndon Johnson, House Speaker Sam Rayburn, key committee chairmen on both sides who, when they voted for you, would usually carry with them the votes of ten or so other congressmen who normally followed their lead, and, finally, younger members and their staffs who clearly were gaining seniority and prestige either through diligent work (like Senator Thomas Kuchel of California) or through their potential candidacy for President (like Senator John Kennedy of Massachusetts).

In all my encounters I tried to impart the feeling to the members and their staffs that I cared about them and that I respected them. (I had learned an important lesson on the eve of the 1956 elections, when, in a meeting at Democratic National Committee headquarters, I ended a report on the likely outcome of the vote in the states I had worked for Kefauver with the remark "It looks like Old Bubblehead is gonna win easy." National Chairman Jim Finnegan glared at me and remonstrated: "I know how you feel. But that is no way to refer to the President of the United States." I never again referred to a federal officeholder with opprobrium—at least, not publicly.)

I would then offer to write speech drafts for members interested in making some remarks on behalf of a labor bill. I felt about writing speeches like Alben Barkley felt about being tarred and feathered. If it wasn't for the honor, he said, he'd as soon walk. But with the help of my wife, Janice, a management counselor named Dick Cooperman, and Stan Seganish, who edited the Retail Clerks' magazine, I managed somehow to turn out reasonably articulate statements that even included a fairly neat phrase now and then. (In one speech for Olin Johnston, I described Eisenhower's proposed "rolling adjustment" as meaning that "the prices get adjusted upward and the farmers and the workingmen get rolled.")

And anytime someone would assist me in writing a speech or gathering material for an official statement, I would make certain that the recipient senator or representative would send that person a signed note of thanks (or an autographed picture for a particularly important project). That would help assure I could call on those same people again for their assistance.

I decided that more than anything, I wanted to be a successful lobbyist. I had been a moderate success as a congressional committee staff man and certainly no more than fair as a practicing attorney. But here was a chance to excel. And to do that, I had to get to know as much as possible about as many congressmen and their aides as possible. If you want to go hunting, you go where the ducks are. Therefore, I decided against depending on the telephone to make my contacts and sell my point of view as too many lobbyists are prone to do. Sure, it would save time. But I didn't believe then or now it succeeds like sitting with a person face to face, sharing a lunch with him, or sipping a cocktail after quitting time or at an evening party.

It was through that kind of personal contact that members came to depend on me, whether it was in connection with their *affaires de coeur* or whether it was a personal crisis. But it also meant I could depend on them to support me in a legislative pinch.

I developed what came to be known as "Chuck's CIA" on Capitol Hill. There was little I didn't know about every key personality in Congress. I started with routine sources like the *Congressional Quarterly* and, later, the *National Journal* to keep up with pet projects of different members. Next I devoured the social pages, which, in Washington, are keys to which congressmen are friendly with what lobbies. Also, it was important to read the official biographies of members in the *Congressional Directory*. The reason is that those biographies are prepared by the members themselves. They thus contain information the congressman wants you to know and what he therefore considers important. Asking a member off-handedly if he has kept up his Masonic ties (when he includes Masonic membership in his biography) or whether he's found time to be active in the local unit of the VFW almost always would turn a light on in his eyes and get him talking about himself—usually a congressman's favorite subject.

I would regularly chat with my contacts in the state or district of a congressman I was planning to call on to pick up little local tidbits about his background, his current political strength, and key local issues with which he was likely to be concerned. (I developed a questionnaire which union leaders around the country would regularly send me keeping me posted on any new developments in the member's relationship with his constituents.)

But all would have been for nothing if I did not wear out a pair of shoes a month treading the halls of Congress to see members and their staffs at every possible opportunity, whether I had anything particular in mind or not. In fact, it was best if I didn't have a program to sell. The visit, merely expressing my interest to say hello and to see if there were anything I could do to be of current service to a member, was always more appreciated than those in which I came on like a traveling salesman trying to unload surplus goods. Then when I had something to sell, it wouldn't seem as if I only turned up when I had a problem.

Most lobbyists arrange their vacations to coincide with congressional recesses, when the members leave Washington and go home for a week or a month. Not me. When Congress goes home, most of the staff members stay behind and continue working to prepare projects that must be ready when the members return. But at least they have more time to spare than they do when a session is in progress. So I use that time to drop around to different offices and take staff people out to lunch. At first, most of them are surprised I would even bother. Then they are astounded to learn I have nothing up my sleeve that I'd like presented to the congressman when he gets back to Washington. Those lunches have paid off tenfold in my ability to get through to a congressman I need to reach no matter how busy the man may be. Having key staff people as your friends is often more important than golfing once a month with the majority leader.

It was through the simple but time-consuming expedient of seeing as many people as possible as often as possible that I was able to achieve that most precious commodity of lobbying— access. Some lobbyists could get it with endless supplies of money. Some could get it because they were personages (like former senators or high-level aides to a former President) in their own right. I had neither enormous financial resources nor was I then or now an "important" person in Washington.

But in time it enabled me to win important victories from the disparate likes of John Kennedy, Lyndon Johnson—and even that symbol of rock-hard conservatism himself, Barry Goldwater.

11

SMELLING LIKE A ROSE

Once, when he was President of the United States, Lyndon Johnson took me aside and said:

"Chuck, you're the only man I know who could fall into a bucket of shit and come up smelling like a rose."

He had in mind the times during his presidency when, with his incendiary temper, he had accused me of screwing up an assignment and then, after he had cooled off, would concede I had done well. At least, most of the time.

The Johnson years, during which he borrowed me frequently from the Retail Clerks (and thus insured me and our union of the greatest possible support at the highest possible level) were, indeed, roselike. But, as in almost everything in politics and lobbying, I didn't just happen into his confidence. If I had not worked diligently to get to know Johnson while he was in the Senate, or if I had abandoned him at the nadir of his influence during his powerless vice-presidential years, he would not have called on me later and I would have missed the opportunity to have the ear of an incumbent President, that wistful dream of all lobbyists.

Not getting to know senators and representatives "when" can often lead to serious embarrassments. Once I walked on an elevator at the Capitol in the company of Senator William Proxmire of my home state of Wisconsin. With us was John Tower of Texas. It was shortly after Tower had come to the Senate in mid-1961 to replace Lyndon Johnson, who had resigned his congressional seat to become Vice-President. Tower, a short man who affected cowboy boots in those days, was not yet widely known among the thousands of young people who work as Senate aides, messengers and elevator operators.

In the elevator, Proxmire asked for the fourth floor and Tower asked for the second. The practice in the Senate is that an elevator operator will first take a senator to his floor no matter who else is aboard. Dutifully, the young operator sped to the fourth floor while Proxmire and I were chatting. As we started to get off, I heard Tower behind us say quietly, "Son, I told you I wanted the second floor."

"Look, cowboy," the youth said harshly, "that other man was a United States Senator."

The door closed then and I don't know what Tower may have replied. But I didn't see that young man around the Senate after that.

While getting to know the members by names and faces (and, more importantly, getting them to know me) was my most important task, the second was to make certain that no member considered me, my union or the labor movement in general as bitter bedrock enemies because we might disagree most of the time. Third, it was vital never to lie to or mislead a member about the relative importance of an issue or our opposition's position and strength. It was self-defeating to cry wolf on each and every proposal supported by labor; if you did, you could bet that few members would walk the extra mile with you on an issue you truly considered significant. And if you tried to suggest, especially to a member from a marginal district, that other conservatives were going to support a particular issue (when, in reality, you didn't know for sure) or to misrepresent the opposition

113

by underplaying its importance in terms of possible future voter reaction, you could count on two things: the member would find out sooner or later, and you would have lost a vote forever. Even worse, he would spread the word that you couldn't be trusted—and you could kiss your career good-by.

Sam Rayburn taught me that. Shortly after I joined the Retail Clerks, I paid him a courtesy call. If he remembered my perfidy at the 1956 Chicago Democratic Convention, he never let on. Instead, he sat me down for a short course in lobby tactics.

"Never," he instructed, "cut anybody off from contact, even if you think your philosophies are like night and day. This year's enemy may turn out to be your strongest ally next year. Times change, constituencies change and members change on issues. And," he added, sternly pointing a finger at me, "never lie. If you take a shit on the fourth floor of the Cannon Office Building, everyone will know about it on the first floor fifteen minutes later."

The same, however, was true for congressmen. When they made a commitment to another member or to a lobbyist on how they would vote on a bill, they were expected to stick to it.

It was through such a commitment made to me by Lyndon Johnson in 1958 that I began developing a relationship of mutual trust and respect that was to last until the day he died.

By that time, the Active Ballot Club of my union had grown strong enough to exercise some political clout, and I had been moving on all eight burners to try to get retail clerks included in a minimum wage bill.

Among the senators who had promised to support me was Johnson, then the Democratic leader in the Senate and widely recognized as perhaps the most influential senator since the days of Clay, Webster and Calhoun. President Eisenhower had realized that he couldn't push a single program through Congress, despite his personal popularity, without Johnson's support. So while he was the single most powerful Democratic officeholder in the country, he was also wooed regularly by the Republican White House.

But Johnson, though he was trying to broaden his political base beyond Texas for a planned run at the presidency himself, was shrewd enough to avoid the pitfalls that Kefauver had encountered by becoming too liberal too fast for his own constituency. He had begun by that time to support a number of labor and civil rights issues. But he reconsidered his pledge to support the retail clerks' movement. Numbers of rich businessmen in Texas who would contribute lavishly to Johnson's national ambitions were opposed to our position and Johnson did not want to alienate them for a relatively small union.

Accordingly, he summoned me to his office one afternoon.

"It's downright embarrassing, Chuck," he said, getting out of his chair and drawing himself to his full, impressive bulk. It seemed to me that whenever he wanted something he always used the sense of authority that somehow surrounds big men when they're standing next to you.

"Can I get off the hook on the minimum wage bill?" he asked, peering down at me.

Obviously, I was troubled. Johnson support would almost guarantee Senate passage. Without it, it would be a toss-up. On the other hand, this man was too powerful a legislator to cross. Sure, I knew he'd stick with me if I insisted on it by telling him how much I had been counting on him and that I had already told other senators and other labor lobbyists of his position. A change would mean going back to everyone I had induced into supporting us on the basis that the majority leader was in our corner. But if I held him to it, I was afraid it might be the last favor he'd ever do for me.

"Leader," I said, "give me a day. If I can pick up a couple of votes that are marginal right now, you're off."

He thanked me and I left. The other votes really didn't matter. We'd get them or we wouldn't. But I wanted Johnson to think I would have a lot of extra work to do because of his decision to renege. That way he'd remember I had done a favor for *him*.

Next day, I reported through one of his top aides, Bobby Baker, that the matter LBJ and I had discussed had been taken care of. A few days later, I got a note from Johnson thanking me for my co-operation.

The fact was that we had blown our chances in the Senate for that year. But we didn't have a prayer then in the House, anyway. I had to balance the psychological boost we would have received by getting the measure through one house (thus setting the stage for complete congressional approval at a later date) against risking the loss of future support from Johnson on this and other labor measures. To be sure, I had a lot of explaining to do among my own people. In the end, though they realized it was a serious risk, they agreed I had done the right thing.

But my friendship with Johnson was cemented later because of a misunderstanding that had ignited his volatile temper.

"What in the goddam hell is this all about?" he shouted at me after he had called me to his office one day. He threw a sheaf of papers at me across the desk. It was a speech by Senator Proxmire in which the maverick Wisconsin Democrat had assailed Johnson and the Democratic leadership in Congress for autocracy, cronyism and arm-twisting tactics. Johnson assumed I had written the speech because I was friendly with my home-state senator and had helped him on numerous occasions.

"I didn't write that speech, Leader," I said.

"You're a goddam liar," he bellowed.

"I'm not. He doesn't need me to write speeches like that. Besides," I mused, "it's a damn good speech. People from Wisconsin like an independent-minded senator."

"Like that shit McCarthy, I suppose."

"McCarthy may have been a lot of things," I said, my provincialism aroused, "but you can't say he wasn't independent-minded."

Johnson started lecturing me on the need for strong congressional leadership and party discipline. He would hunch over me, push his face down close to mine and when, of necessity, I took a step back, he'd move forward again like a tiger stalking its prey. When I could slip a word in edgewise, I would say that I agreed, and repeat that I hadn't written the speech.

When Bobby Baker walked in the room, I felt a sense of relief. He started out again as soon as he saw the argument going on, but I stopped him.

"Bobby, will you tell this man that I didn't write that Proxmire speech?"

"Well?" Johnson demanded, glancing at Baker.

"I don't want to get in the middle of this," Baker said, and started out again.

"Please, Bobby," I pleaded, knowing how highly Johnson valued his opinion. "Tell him if you think I wrote this thing."

"Well," Baker said deliberately, "I'll say this, Senator. If Lipsen says he didn't write it, he didn't write it. Besides"—he grinned—"with all the publicity it got, he'd be braggin' about it all over the Hill. I'd've heard about it by now."

Johnson looked at both of us for a moment.

"Okay," he said. "You're right and I'm wrong. Lipsen, from now on, you're my expert on labor."

I was elated. To be sure, I knew that Johnson loved to spread hyperbole over nearly all his political acquaintances. He would attract people by the strength of his personality and later would retain their loyalty by alternating a tongue-lashing with a clearly outlandish compliment, like telling them they were his number-one this or his top expert or confidant on that. But I knew from that day he would listen to my advice. He wouldn't always take it, and I knew he would value more highly the advice of many people other than myself. But I would have access to one of America's most politically potent men, and that's what counted for a lobbyist.

Baker, of course, would fall on hard times in the years ahead. His acceptance of kickbacks from businessmen in return for his influence while he was a top employee in the Senate would not only disgrace him but result in a jail sentence. Still, I always admired and respected him for his political acumen and his loyalty to his friends. I also admired, in a rather awe-struck way, his uncanny ability to juggle a long string of girl friends without seemingly getting them, or his wife at the time, angry with him.

"Bobby," I asked one day while we were tippling at the Quorum Club, a now defunct hangout for high-level Democrats that Bobby had organized, "how the hell do you get away with murder?"

"Well, Chuck," he drawled, "I know there's nothing worse than a woman scorned. It's a problem, all right."

"Doesn't anyone ever blow the whistle on you?"

"No."

117

"How do you get away with it?" I insisted.

"Well, I'll share a little secret with you." He leaned closer to me. "You're goin' with a girl but then you meet somebody else. You don't want to get her sore. After all, I'm in the public eye these days. Besides, I don't want her callin' my wife or anythin'. It'd be embarrassing, to say the least."

"So?"

"So," he continued, "you don't dump her right away. What you do is when you go out, you pick your nose at the table. When you're walkin' you scratch your balls or break wind. You eat garlic and belch. Maybe you even skip a bath for a day or two. Pretty soon, when you call her for a date, she says she can't, an old girl friend or cousin has just come to town. You try again and it's the same thing. Then you don't have to call anymore. They never tell anybody anything—and they never give you any trouble. I mean, what self-respectin' woman wants it known she'd been goin' around with one of the biggest slobs in Washington?"

In the ensuing years, both Johnson and Speaker Rayburn taught me how to keep out of trouble with congressmen. "If you want to get along, go along" was Rayburn's favorite cliché. They both taught me that the essence of political leadership was recognizing that congressmen had a primary duty—for their electability if not to fulfill a constitutional obligation—to vote their districts; that is, to vote the way they thought their constituents wanted them to vote, especially on crucial back-home issues. But when a particular vote was only of passing interest to their constituents, a congressman should be bent six ways from Sunday, even if it violated his conscience, to vote the way the party leadership told him to.

From time to time, the pot could be sweetened by seeing to it that a congressman who went along, even against his better judgment, was handed a pork barrel project for his district. Even on federal projects that were to be approved at the bureaucratic level, a system was devised to give voters the impression their congressman was responsible for getting them. Every agency that was responsible for approving dams, roads, military installations, federal buildings or anything that would infuse a community with some new economic benefit was instructed to pass the news not to the public but, rather, to a friendly senator or congressman in whose district or state the project would be built. The member would then announce the good news to the press and the resulting publicity was certain to hammer another nail in the coffin of any likely political opponent.

Perhaps the classic story relating to how that system worked came from an incident some years later, when Johnson was President and was pushing ahead on his disastrous course in Vietnam. It was early in the war and only a few senators like Vance Hartke, Ernest Gruening, Wayne Morse and William Fulbright were beginning to break ranks from the general congressional support of the war policy. One who was growing shaky was Senator Frank Church of Idaho. At a White House cocktail party, Johnson sidled up to Church.

"I understand," he said, "you're thinking of making a speech against my policy in Vietnam [pronounced by Johnson as VEET-nam]."

"Well, Mr. President," Church replied, "I've been talking to Walter Lippmann [the renowned columnist] about that. He's convinced me that it's a self-defeating policy, that it's basically a civil war and the people we're supporting are an anti-democratic lot."

"That's fine, Frank," Johnson said, "but you listen here. The next time you want a dam in Idaho, you go talk to Walter Lippmann about it and see how much he can help you."

Johnson was a man who not only knew and liked to use every lever of power available to him as a senator or as President, but he also gloried in lording his greater power over others, perhaps to swell his ego or because the appearance of power, in fact, added to it.

There is, for example, the story that during the inaugural parade on January 20, 1965, Johnson leaned over from his place in the presidential viewing booth toward the new Vice-President, Hubert Humphrey, and whispered: "Hubert, in case you don't know it, I've got your balls in my pocket."

After he took over as President in November of 1963, Johnson frequently invited lawmakers to the White House swimming pool (later filled in by Nixon) and insisted they all go "skinny-dipping." "The idea," says William Miller, the Republican national chairman who ran for Vice-President in 1964 before dropping into oblivion to be rescued recently by an American Express television commercial, "was to get everybody naked and put them on the defensive. He knew that if you took away somebody's clothes, you took away their protective outer defenses."

And even in small perquisites, Johnson liked to be number one. When Johnson was President, the tables had been somewhat turned on him in terms of his need for the support of the opposition party's leader to push through key programs. While Eisenhower depended on Johnson's support when LBJ was Senate majority leader, Johnson needed the backing of Everett McKinley Dirksen of Illinois, the Republican leader in the Senate. Dirksen became a legend in his own time, especially by gaining credit for Johnsonian civil rights programs because without his support, it was believed the Administration programs would have no chance of passing.

Johnson knew the necessity of suffering—even promoting— publicity for Dirksen. But he didn't have to like it. He took succor in the regality of his office, in "summoning" Dirksen to the White House. Earlier, he found other ways to try to remind Dirksen of their relative places in the Washington pecking order, when Johnson was majority leader of the Senate and Dirksen the minority leader.

One way was believed to be through Johnson's limousine telephone. The story may be apocryphal, but it is worth retelling. While Dirksen, as Senate minority leader, was assigned a limousine, it did not come equipped with a mobile phone like the majority leader's. Whenever possible, the story goes, Johnson would telephone Dirksen from his car. He would invariably call at the lunch hour, hoping Dirksen would not be in his office, and would have to be summoned to call immediately about some legislative matter. Johnson knew Dirksen would like that; he would probably be lunching with an important constituent who would be terribly impressed when his senator was called from the lunch table because he had urgent business.

But when Dirksen would receive the message, it would invariably include the number for Johnson's mobile phone. Johnson, on receiving Dirksen's return call, would usually say something like, "I'm sorry to trouble you, Ev, but actually I'm en route to an important meeting and I might not have had time to get in touch with you. So I figured I could catch you while I was in my car."

Dirksen, who knew the importance of one-upmanship in Washington at least as well as Johnson did, took appropriate counter-measures. He pushed through an appropriation for himself and other Republican leaders in the House and Senate for telephones in their limousines on the premise they, too, might be needed in the event of a legislative emergency.

As soon as his phone was installed, Dirksen had his chauffeur take him out for a spin and he telephoned Johnson at his Senate office.

"Excuse me, Lyndon," he began, "but I had this matter that I thought I should talk to you about right away. In fact, I'm calling from my car telephone."

Whatever the call was about, Johnson knew it was far less important to Dirksen than letting him know that the Senate Republican leader also had a telephone in his limousine. So Johnson ordered a counter-measure.

Two days later, Johnson was out for a spin in his limo and, at about the lunch hour, he placed a call to Dirksen. Sure enough, Dirksen was not in and would return the call promptly.

Ten minutes later, the call was returned. Johnson waited a moment and then took the receiver.

"Lyndon," Dirksen said in his mellifluous, gravelly voice. "It's Ev Dirksen returning your call."

"Oh, yes, Ev," Johnson said. "Thanks for calling so promptly." Then he waited a moment and said to an imagined companion, "What's that? Oh, yes." He turned back to the receiver and said: "Ev? Lyndon again. Excuse me while I put you on hold. I've got to take a call on my *other* phone."

With that, Johnson put the call on hold before bellowing with laughter. One-upmanship. Johnson was a master.

There was never a question in my mind as we moved toward the Democratic National Convention of 1960 that the Retail

Clerks, unlike much of the labor movement, should support the candidacy of Lyndon Johnson for President.

There were a couple of reasons. First, my boss, Jim Suffridge, a liberal Republican who had liked Kefauver, felt comfortable with Johnson but hated Kennedy as the antithesis of everything he believed in as a Southern Protestant Republican. Second, I was already tabbed as anti-Kennedy by his tight little group of supporters because I had supported Kefauver for Vice-President in 1956 (assuming, as one could never do with the Kennedys, that he had forgotten our run-in at the 1952 convention, which would only increase his antipathy toward me). Third, I had persuaded Suffridge (rather easily) that the union's best bet was to go with Johnson. If he won the nomination, he'd be the candidate and possibly the next President of the United States. If he lost, he'd still be the majority leader of the Senate. On the off chance that Kennedy would win the nomination and somehow be able to defeat Nixon in November, it was likely that he would still have to support general labor legislation and that Johnson would still be a more potent force than the President in pushing legislation through the Congress.

But there was another reason which gave us pause in any notion we might have had to support Kennedy for President. Suffridge had recently uncovered a scandal within our Retail Clerks' local chapter in Detroit. The local was one of our largest, paying about five dollars a month dues per person to the national union based on a membership of some 10,000. We had received reports indicating our membership there was much larger, and when we looked into the discrepancy, we discovered that the local leaders were not retail clerks at all, but former Teamsters controlled by Teamster boss Jimmy Hoffa. The fact was there were about 20,000 members in Detroit. While we should have been receiving some $100,000 a month, we were getting just about half that amount. While we couldn't prove it, we believed that the Teamsters were raking off the difference and kicking some of it back to their hacks who were running our union.

Suffridge reacted by putting the local union under trusteeship, a union ploy which gave operating power to the national organization and took it away from the local officers pending resolution of the difficulties which prompted the action. He was careful, however, not to say why—at least, not for public consumption. However unpopular Hoffa was in the national mind, it still would do the Retail Clerks no good for the world to know that Hoffa was trying to take us over, even one local.

But the news of the action did not escape the hawk eye of a young counsel to Senator John McClellan's committee investigating unions—in particular, the Teamsters Union.

Young Bobby Kennedy called me and asked to get together with me and with Sol Lippman, general counsel for the Retail Clerks. He wanted details of Hoffa's involvement with our Detroit local, especially anything that would indicate Hoffa was raking off as much as $50,000 a month for himself or his union.

I agreed, and a couple of days later Kennedy, accompanied by Pierre Salinger, then one of his investigators, met with us at our offices. Lippman, a nervous man, agreed to help Kennedy—but on the condition he not be summoned to testify publicly. "Good heavens!" Lippman said over and over, slapping his hand to his forehead. "I'd be dead in the labor movement if I testified."

Kennedy agreed and, through us, was able to collect enough information to provide significant leads on Hoffa's possible personal involvement in a rake-off. (Lippman may have been playing both sides against the middle. Years later, when Hoffa was in prison, Lippman served as a contact with him in Hoffa's efforts to show collusion between the White House and Frank Fitzsimmons, Hoffa's successor at the Teamsters, to keep Hoffa from playing an active role in union activities.)

But despite his promise, Kennedy called back a few days later and said he was planning to subpoena Lippman. The lawyer was sweating. "You don't need me to hang Hoffa," Lippman pleaded. "You must have a very weak case if you need me."

I grabbed the phone from Lippman. "Okay, you son of a bitch," I hollered into the mouthpiece. "You call Sol to testify and I'll come as his counsel. And then I'll point out to the press and the world that Bobby Kennedy is a fucking liar—that he promised not to call this man because it would wreck his career and then turned around and did it anyway."

Kennedy never called Lippman. And while it was not until he

was Attorney General that Bobby was able to put Hoffa behind bars, the McClellan hearings paved the way by implanting in the public mind the idea that Hoffa was a national scourge.

So again I had crossed swords with the Kennedys and while I did not have the inclination to support Jack for President, I was at least equally certain he would not be especially interested in having me directly involved with his campaign.

So Lyndon Johnson was our choice. For a while, many of us, including Johnson, thought he had a chance to wrest the nomination away from Kennedy, especially if Hubert Humphrey was able to inflict some damage on the Massachusetts senator in the West Virginia and Wisconsin primaries.

Flying with Johnson during a campaign trip, Walter Cronkite of CBS asked the Texan whom he thought would make the best President.

"Me," Johnson answered unhesitatingly. "I'm the most qualified in international affairs, domestic issues and in politics."

"What do you think about Senator Kennedy?" Cronkite asked.

"He's bright," Johnson said. "But he's like a yearling bull. He sees all these cows and thinks he can take care of all of them. But then he runs out of gas after one or two. That's how he is on the issues. He's a visionary. He'll find out you've got to know a hell of a lot about practical politics if you want to get anything done."

"What about Humphrey?" Cronkite continued.

"Hubert," Johnson said, "is a great senator who's got his tongue and his mind synchronized. But he just talks too much. He's like a little boy sitting on the curb playing with himself. He knows he shouldn't do it, but it feels so good he just can't stop."

By the time he got to Los Angeles, though, Johnson knew it was all over. Kennedy had made a powerful showing in the primaries and Johnson's only chance had been based on a relatively even race between Humphrey and Kennedy. What happened next—Kennedy's decision to ask Johnson to be his vice-presidential candidate—demonstrated, however, that the yearling bull knew a thing or two about practical politics after all. Johnson's decision to accept disturbed me, of course, because it might push me beyond the pale. Not only had I opposed Kennedy in the nominating process, but I had done so in the belief that with Johnson as Senate leader, I'd still have a powerfully influential friend. But with LBJ buried in the vice-presidency, I might end up at square one with a hostile President and a new majority leader to cultivate. (Johnson's shrewd decision to run simultaneously for re-election to the U. S. Senate from Texas as a hedge against his possible defeat on the national ticket was hardly comforting. I feared a Nixon victory more than the problem of somehow making my peace with a President Kennedy. I remembered Sam Rayburn telling me that one of the few members of the House he never liked was "Tricky Dick." "If Leonardo was painting the Last Supper today," Rayburn said, "he'd use Nixon as a model for Judas.")

But not all my hopes were dashed. When we returned to Washington for a rump session of the Congress, Johnson called.

"On that minimum wage bill?" he asked rhetorically. "The one I got off of a while back?"

"I remember," I said.

"I want back on."

"We might have enough without you, Leader," I said.

"I want back on," he repeated.

"Including my people?" I asked, meaning retail clerks, then not entitled to a minimum wage under federal law.

"All the way," he said.

Johnson now had a national constituency to play to, and he was trying to liberalize his voting record as fully as possible.

The next step was getting Kennedy nailed down on the bill. It was no easy task. For one thing, Kennedy was the Democratic nominee for President. Everyone and his brother was trying to get his ear. For another, he wanted to return to the Senate as the Democratic leader now that he was the party's nominee, and he had a number of issues on which he would try to capture national attention while Nixon was trapped in the vice-presidency. Finally, including retail clerks in a minimum wage bill was far from universally popular even in the labor movement. The so-called Mom and Pop stores were vehemently opposed on grounds such a law would put them out of business. Besides, a number of labor leaders, recognizing our membership represented only a fraction of the retail workers around the country, didn't like the idea of providing significant benefits for people who were opposing unionization as well as those who already had joined the union.

My reasoning was that we had to get a foot in the door. If we provided a union-sponsored minimum wage, we could use that as an arguing point in trying to recruit new members. Additionally, we could offer insurance and retirement benefits. And we could argue that the more members we had, the better the chances of increasing general minimum wage benefits in the future. But it wouldn't matter a damn to us what the Congress did regarding minimum wages if retail clerks weren't included on the bill.

I was pleasantly surprised when Kennedy granted me an audience. It had been arranged through the good offices of Arthur Goldberg, then general counsel for the United Steelworkers.

"Arthur tells me you want the retail clerks included on the bill," he said tersely in his Senate office one afternoon.

"Yes, sir," I answered. "The Senate's already approved it and it looks like clear sailing in the House."

"You're in," he said without hesitating.

"Thank you, Senator," I answered.

"I'll need help from you guys," he added.

"You'd get it anyway," I said truthfully.

"I know that," he said. "I mean I want you to bust your balls."

"We'd have done that, too."

"We'll see," he said, smiling.

There was work to do, but it looked good. With both Kennedy and Johnson behind us, I saw no way we could fail.

Actually, our big breakthrough had come months before, when we had succeeded in getting a bill including retail clerks reported favorably from the Senate Labor and Public Welfare Committee. From our count, the committee was evenly split over the inclusion of retail clerks. The problem was not that we had a shortage of liberals; it was that a number of the liberals had been discouraged from including us by the lobbyists for the parent AFL-CIO. They wouldn't admit it openly, but they were among those who considered a white-collar union somehow less

126

than worthy—especially when so many non-unionists would profit from being handed a minimum wage. Jack Kennedy, for one, was among those who, before the convention in Los Angeles, had not supported us.

It had been my view that with friends like Jack Kennedy, labor needed no enemies. The previous year, in 1959, Kennedy had ruined us on the Landrum-Griffin bill (which I had been calling the Kennedy-Landrum-Griffin bill, especially to labor groups which I had been trying to turn to Lyndon Johnson).

He had decided to take the lead at a Senate-House conference committee on the bill in an attempt to come up with something closer to labor's wishes than the bill that had been passed by the House. But he was regularly outfoxed by the more seasoned old hands, like Graham Barden of North Carolina, who supported a tough anti-labor bill.

Barden knew the intricacies of Landrum-Griffin inside out. But every time he'd raise a specific point, Kennedy would turn for advice to the staff attorney he had accompanying him for the occasion, a Harvard professor of law named Archibald Cox (who would become the nation's first special prosecutor probing the Watergate scandals).

Barden knew how to twist a dirk in someone's side. He would ask a question and before Kennedy could respond Barden would say: "Of co'se, ah don't expect you to answer till you check with the perfesser."

Finally, Kennedy exploded. "Goddammit, Congressman," he spat one afternoon, "cut this shit out. And don't pick on Archie. He's one of the most brilliant lawyers in the country. Besides," he added, "I can answer your questions myself."

"Well, then," Barden said, the soul of southern courtliness, "we won't need the perfesser anymore. Perhaps he'd like to leave."

To save face, Kennedy told Archie to go. As soon as he did, Barden engineered a couple of quick votes to retain some of the most stringent portions of the bill. The upshot was that Kennedy, as chairman of the conference, was put in the position of having to support a bill then viewed by organized labor as a death knell. It was hardly that, as time demonstrated. But at the time, it seemed clearly evil. If Kennedy had been running against anyone except Nixon that year (especially if Nelson Rockefeller had somehow won his party's nomination) I don't think organized labor would have supported him.

In any event, I couldn't count on Kennedy in early 1960 to give me that extra vote I needed to assure that the Senate committee would approve a bill including retail clerks.

On an educated gamble, I settled on Barry Goldwater as my choice. Until then, Goldwater had, as might have been expected, opposed putting retail clerks in a minimum wage bill. Indeed, he was generally opposed to any pro-labor legislation. He agreed to see me, he said later, because when I had paid him a visit in 1958, I was the first labor lobbyist even to bother to see him regarding any issue.

I told him I needed his vote in committee or retail clerks wouldn't have a prayer of being included in a bill that year.

He listened patiently as I made my pitch.

"I'm against it, Chuck," he said simply. "And I'll tell you something else," he added, his voice rising. "I've been damned angry at the union boys who've tried to bully me."

"What do you mean?" I asked, puzzled.

"Some of your people have been spreading the word that I'm against putting the retail clerks in the bill because I own a department store and want to keep the lid on my employees' wages. It's a damned lie and they know it."

"I can't believe it," I said, believing every word. "Everyone knows you don't own the store anymore."

"Not everyone," he groused. "You know it. I know it. But do the people know it?"

I thought a moment. "Senator," I said firmly, "I promise you that I'll put a stop to this immediately. No senator—but especially not a man of your integrity—ought to be subjected to that kind of whispering campaign."

I rose to leave but he waved me down.

"Look," he said, "I don't like this new bill and you know it. But one thing does make sense. If the Senate takes it up, it ought to have the opportunity to decide if your people should be a part of the law. I'll tell you what I'll do," he said, slapping his hand on the desk with finality. "I'll vote for it in committee. But I reserve the right to oppose it when it reaches the floor."

"I think that's very fair, Senator," I said, and then bid him good-by.

I could barely contain myself. I knew I had the votes to get the bill through the full Senate once it reached the floor. Goldwater didn't know that. My problem was getting the thing out of committee. With Goldwater's vote, that was taken care of. I turned the corner of the Senate corridor after leaving his office and then I let out a joyous whoop. A Capitol policeman glared at me as if I were a nut. Before he could ask me what the hell I was up to, I walked to him and said, apologetically, that I had just gotten some good news.

"I didn't mean to make a racket," I said, grinning like a madman. He kept glaring. "Anyway, I'm just leaving the building."

"See that you do."

I saw Goldwater frequently after that, but he never mentioned his unwitting role in getting the bill passed. Nearly a decade later, though, I received a telephone call from a Goldwater supporter. It was early 1969. By then, of course, the caller knew me not just as a labor lobbyist but also as a man who had been an adviser and advance man for Lyndon Johnson from the 1964 campaign through the end of his term. A Goldwater friend, I most clearly was not.

The call, therefore, was something of a surprise.

"I have a favor to ask," he said evenly. "Barry's son is running for Congress in a special election in California. He needs some help."

What can I do?" I asked warily.

"He needs some money," the Goldwater supporter said. "If he can come on strong with TV commercials he's got a good chance to win."

"Consider it done," I said.

Can you imagine that? A labor lobbyist who was part of the Johnson camp raising money for the son of one of the strongest conservatives ever to walk the halls of Congress? And if Barry, Jr., came to the House, how many pro-labor votes could he be expected to make in his lifetime? Two? One? None? Probably the last. But here was a Goldwater man asking me to get money to elect the Senator's boy to the House of Representatives. And here was Chuck Lipsen doing just that. I called a number of my friends on the Coast. Most were businessmen who maintained good relations with organized labor because they figured meeting reasonable wage and fringe-benefit demands was a lot cheaper than facing an annual strike. I told them I would answer no questions, but could they get a couple of thousand to young Barry Goldwater running for Congress out there? They agreed almost to a man and we ended up funneling more than $10,000 into his campaign, more than enough to give him the edge he needed.

Goldwater never mentioned it to me. I never again heard from the caller. And I keep telling myself there was no *quid pro quo*. After all, nearly ten years had passed since Goldwater had done me a favor. And there was no indication that he knew of the favor asked in return.

But if Goldwater had not, in fact, crucially helped the Retail Clerks union, no matter how inadvertently, would a supporter of his even have thought to call me, a labor lobbyist known as a liberal Democrat, to help elect Goldwater's conservative Republican son? And even if Goldwater himself had called, would I have agreed to do so if I had not known that without his help when I needed it my cause would have been lost? It's hard, if not impossible, to define a *quid pro quo*. No matter. I'm glad I did it then. I would do it again today.

With Jack Kennedy, though, perhaps because of the great pressure on him both as presidential candidate and as the suddenly endowed Democratic leader of the Senate, his word proved to be less than binding.

By the time the 1960 political conventions were over, the House had passed a minimum wage bill. But it had not cleared the Senate and no one was sure whether there would be time for a Senate-House conference committee to iron out the differences. Finally, the laundered conference bill would need approval by both houses again. Even if a bill were passed, the retail clerks could be dropped from it anywhere along the line. We were vulnerable because we were new to the minimum wage, and we were doubly jeopardized by the knowledge among congressmen that many people promoting the general bill didn't especially care if were included or not.

Nonetheless, close to midnight on a fall evening on which the Senate was debating the bill, I wearily decided it was safe to leave and go home. Kennedy was leading the debate on the floor and we had survived the conference committee decisions to change a point or two. We were in—or so it seemed.

As I settled into a steaming tub, my wife rapped at the bathroom door.

"It's Arthur Goldberg on the phone. He says it's urgent."

"Oh, shit," I muttered. "What the hell can be so important?"

"Beats me," Janice said. "It's nearly one o'clock in the morning."

"Okay, okay. Tell him to hold a minute while I dry off."

I was still dripping when I picked up an extension phone in the bedroom.

"What's happening, Arthur?" I asked.

"Nothing except your friend Jack Kennedy is about to do you in."

"*My* friend? I thought he was *your* buddy."

"Let's not argue the point," Goldberg said. "*Our* friend is about to sell you out. He's agreed to drop the retail clerks from the bill."

"How the hell can he do that?"

"Damned if I know," Goldberg said. "Maybe he's just scratching through the language with a pencil."

"Okay, Arthur," I sighed, "don't be cute. I'll get there in twenty minutes."

I must have broken every traffic law in the Washington metropolitan area, but I reached the tiled foyer outside the Senate floor in seventeen minutes flat.

The debate was still in progress and I handed a messenger a note asking Senator Kennedy to see me. (No one but a senator or specially selected staff members is permitted on the floor; lobbyists and constituents must wait in the foyer for a member to leave the floor and meet them outside the chamber.)

Meanwhile, I asked some of my cronies hanging around if they knew what was happening regarding the retail clerks. One of them said he had understood that Kennedy had made a deal with the building trades unions to include, at the last minute, a section permitting situs picketing. (Situs picketing, then outlawed, permitted putting up a picket line at a construction site if any of the several building trades unions went out on strike. The result would likely be that none of the trade unionists would cross the line and construction would then be forced to halt. Companies were obviously opposed to it because with only one or even two unions out, they could probably keep construction going.)

But, my friend added, he didn't know why Kennedy was dropping us from the bill—unless, of course, he thought he could slip situs picketing through only on condition he drop one or more sections from the committee-passed version.

That had to be it, I thought. The rat was selling us out because he would rather accommodate the larger, far more affluent building trades boys, most of whom tended toward the Republicans anyway. If he could get them in the bill, they would give his campaign hundreds of thousands of dollars that might otherwise have gone to Nixon. They were, to be sure, a bigger political plum than the Retail Clerks International Association.

But the bastard had given his word and he was about to break it.

By the time he came off the floor, he was visibly weary. But I didn't give him a chance to speak.

"What the hell are you doing to me?" I demanded. "You're dropping us for those fucking bad-ass Republican bastards—and I think you owe me an explanation."

That touched him off. "I don't owe you a goddam thing," he shot back. "Give you bastards a finger and then you want an arm." He wheeled and headed back to the floor.

I sighed. To put it mildly, I hadn't handled it well. Chalk up another black mark for Lipsen with the man who might be the next President. I slumped down in a chair and held my head in my hands. When the story got back about how I had screamed at the Democratic presidential nominee in spitting distance from the Senate floor, my goose would be cooked. The Retail Clerks, in the interests of party and labor harmony, would have to let me go. And Jack Kennedy wouldn't have Lipsen to kick around anymore.

When I finished licking my wounds I got up and started to go. Then I heard him calling me.

"Wait a minute, Lipsen," Kennedy said, returning from the chamber. "Look, I'm dead tired. I've been running around this country and we've just come back from the convention. I haven't had a good night's sleep in weeks."

He reached out and touched my shoulder. That was a good sign. None of the Kennedys, as I had known them, were touchers or liked to be touched themselves. "I gave you my word. I'll stick to it. You'll be on the bill."

He didn't wait for my thank-you. He just turned and walked back to the Senate floor.

Sure enough, we made it. Though the bill did not survive a late-year conference committee effort to enact it, Senate action provided the momentum we needed to get it passed in early 1961. For the first time, retail clerks became subject to minimum wage laws and we were on our way to moving from twelfth position among AFL-CIO unions to fifth-largest.

I didn't see much of Jack Kennedy after that. I helped raise money for him in his successful campaign and I was traumatized, like most of the nation, by his murder.

But I never forgot him. It had taken some doing, but he had kept his word, even at the risk of losing support from the building trades. That's really all I ever asked from a politician. And when he came through for me, it was vitally important.

But an old reliable like Lyndon Johnson, he wasn't.

12

SIPPING KAVA-KAVA
IN A LAVA-LAVA

The incredible electricity that John Kennedy generated through the country from the White House shoved Lyndon Johnson into virtual obscurity. Programs like the Peace Corps and proposals for Medicare, civil rights and aid to education brought a rush of intellectuals and pseudo-intellectuals to the capital to "get the country moving again." Tough jawboning of the steel industry infused workingmen with the idea that government was on their side again. And the town reveled in the Kennedy parties and the new attention to culture.

Critics maintain that the aura of Camelot surrounding Kennedy's thousand days as President was a fraud, partly because he succeeded in pushing so few meaningful proposals through Congress and partly because of rumors and allegations concerning Kennedy's overactive libido. There may be some truth in both judgments. Young Senator Kennedy had been considered among the capital's most notorious—and successful—ladies' men in earlier days, and there is no reason to think Jack Kennedy changed his habits overnight. And it was left to Johnson to win enactment of nearly all the Kennedy programs.

But it is too easy to write off the Kennedy years as mere facade. There was something pervasive and real about the way he made Americans feel toward their government and themselves. He somehow radiated a sense of confidence in the land and its people that had never existed before and certainly hasn't since. He made us proud of ourselves and our country, a feeling which Pat Moynihan, with the same Irish wit and outrage at inequality, tried, in a small way, to resurrect not long ago at the United Nations.

The point for me, however, was that Kennedy overshadowed Johnson and his breed of practical politicians to the point of reducing them to nonentities in Washington in the early 1960s. Nobody who was anybody in those days would be caught dead breaking bread with the Vice-President. The Kennedys viewed any Johnsonian with disdain, while Johnson thought any friend of the Massachusetts Mafia was a traitor. I had no real problem, however, since I had backed the wrong horse. I was nobody who was anybody. Even if I didn't want to, I had no choice but to stay with Lyndon Johnson if I was to stay with anybody.

The fact was that Johnson spent most of his time in those days hanging around Capitol Hill and the scenes of his past power. He could be found downing Cutty Sark in the office of Hale Boggs of Louisiana or dropping in on old Senate cronies. Whenever possible, I would call on him and shoot the breeze about current legislative problems. Before he'd embark on a domestic trip, he would phone me and ask for names of labor leaders he should call on, or whether any local labor problems existed in the town or state he was to visit.

But there was little that Johnson could or needed to do for labor in those days. Arthur Goldberg was ensconced as Secretary of Labor, Bobby Kennedy as Attorney General was leading the civil rights push, and Abe Ribicoff took over aid to education and Medicare proposals as Secretary of Health, Education and Welfare. They were halcyon days for nearly everyone in government, and nearly everyone in the labor movement who had supported Kennedy. Notably, that didn't include Lyndon Johnson and it certainly didn't include me.

Still, that didn't hurt our union. We reaped the general benefits that accrued to working men and women, especially from the dwindling unemployment rate. But my loss of status was real. For the first time in eight years, there were dozens of key labor lobbyists with a pipeline to the White House. I was not among them. Labor leaders were consulted on a host of crucial matters by the Administration: is such-and-such a business or industry responsive to labor, or should we lean on it? Is Mister So-and-So the kind of guy you'd like to see ambassador to Bali Ha'i? Which congressmen would you like to see us work for hardest when it comes to re-election? Of course, there were numerous inputs to the White House besides those of labor, and our advice, support or opposition wouldn't necessarily make a difference to a final decision. But for those who were asked their views, the implications were enormous. Not only could they help labor in general but they became highly important people in their own right. By being able to give advice about businessmen, potential diplomats and congressmen, they were sought after by those people who wanted a good word put in. Conversely, by dispensing favors, they were owed many which they could and did collect over the ensuing years.

My time came when Johnson became President after the tragedy at Dallas.

I was driving past the Senate Office Building on that November 22 when the car in front of me stopped suddenly. A man whom I recognized at once as Henry Giugni, the administrative assistant to Senator Daniel Inouye of Hawaii, jumped out of the car and started gawking about crazily. I jumped out of my car.

"Henry," I called. "You all right?"

"Lipsen, for Christ's sake! Come here! Come here quick!"

I rushed to him, not knowing what the hell was going on.

"Have you heard?" he asked, his face tight and contorted.

"Heard what?"

"Get in," he said. We slid into the front seat of his Valiant, with both cars double-parked. His radio was turned up almost deafeningly. ". . . President Kennedy has been shot," the news-caster was saying. "We don't know his condition . . ."

We sat silently, looking at one another in disbelief, listening to the sketchy reports in shocked fascination. I almost didn't notice the man who opened the rear door and sat behind us to listen, too. I half turned and saw it was Senator Edward Kennedy. He had been presiding in the Senate when someone gave him the word. He must have walked aimlessly from the Capitol toward his office when he spotted us and wanted to get the latest report. Then the announcement came, the announcement that we all knew was imminent.

"Three words tell the story of this tragic day," the newscaster said. "Three words: 'President Kennedy dead.'"

We all looked at one another. Instinctively, I grabbed Kennedy's forearm and squeezed. He nodded. Then he silently slipped out of the car and walked slowly away. In that moment, any hostility I ever had felt toward the Kennedys because of my clashes with Jack and Bobby melted away. The enormous void I suddenly felt at the loss of President Kennedy persuaded me that he had, indeed, created something great in this nation that only sheer blindness could fail to perceive. Whatever the ascension of Johnson would mean to me personally, I knew he could never in-still that same sense of warmth and love in the American people.

The circumstances of the President's death, however ghastly, were peculiarly suited to Johnson's talents. None of the major domestic programs of the Kennedy administration had gotten off dead center. But Johnson was, by nature, a doer and not a thinker. Here was an opportunity to push through Congress per-haps the most ambitious domestic program since the New Deal, and he attacked the problem with relish.

Eventually, after a decent period of mourning, he pushed the intellects back to the college campuses and brought in his own kind of team—men with knowledge of and liking for practical politics. It's true that he always yearned for some kind of bless-ing from academia. But it's just as true those people made him uncomfortable and he would as soon be without them.

As soon as he could do so without seeming crass, Johnson started planning for his election campaign of 1964, and he summoned me from the Retail Clerks to take over a chunk of his advance work. I brought with me a team of workers. My sister, Esther Coopersmith, and my wife, Janice, agreed to take charge of planning Texas-style fund-raising barbecues over the country under the aegis of the Young Citizens for Johnson, which was chaired by Senator Birch Bayh of Indiana. It was important to Johnson that young people flock to his banner with the same enthusiasm they had demonstrated for Jack Kennedy. They never would, of course—but through the Young Citizens, they gave the appearance they were doing so. The barbecues which attracted lawyers and doctors and other professionals in their mid-thirties and early forties were an integral part of creating the impression Johnson had sought.

And I also volunteered the services of my younger brother, Zel, to do advance work for Hubert Humphrey after Humphrey became Johnson's running mate.

The Retail Clerks were ecstatic. To be sure, they would be paying me a salary which I would earn by working more for Johnson than for them. But they knew there would be a pot of gold at the end of a rainbow created by Johnson's election. And Johnson would develop solid relations with many people in the labor movement, especially those running far bigger and richer and more powerful unions than mine. But we were back in again, and that's what counted.

The year was a blur of traversing the country to set up rallies for President Johnson. Most of them came and went without incident. But hardly all.

Johnson agreed to become the first incumbent President ever to visit the Catskill Mountains, those lovely New York hills which hid the mysteries of Washington Irving in an earlier time and had since become the Borscht Belt vacation haven for city dwellers and training ground for young comedians. At the invitation of Joe Resnick, a candidate for Congress, Johnson would dedicate a hospital at Ellenville, New York, and would spend the night at the local resort called the Nevele Country Club. The problem was that the place was jammed and to make room for the President and his entourage, it seemed clear that some reservations would have to be canceled.

Johnson issued orders that he would rather cancel his trip than force anyone to cancel a reservation. "That's a honeymoon place," Johnson said. "All I need is a story to get out that I kept some young couple from celebrating their wedding night."

But in talking to Charles Slutsky, the hotel's proprietor, I was assured that in the normal course of events, there were certain to be more than enough cancellations to accommodate the President. For the time, I put aside that problem. The next hurdle, though, was that the bed in the room to which Johnson would be assigned would be too short for the President's bulk.

"But the only place I can get another bed is in New York City," Slutsky complained. "That's the only place I can find one long enough. It'll cost me a fortune to buy it special and get it delivered up here."

But at my insistence that unless he had a seven-foot-long bed for Johnson the trip would be canceled, Slutsky proceeded. Slutsky knew that the outlay would be more than justified by the enormous publicity generated by the presence of the President. But I had another idea. I suggested that after the trip, Slutsky auction it off, keep enough to cover the cost and shipping, and donate the rest to the new community hospital that Johnson would be there to dedicate. Later, he took my advice and auctioned the bed Johnson had slept in for $5,000.

By the time Johnson arrived, there seemed to be nothing but smooth sailing ahead. But I quickly ran into trouble with him at breakfast.

"What the hell is this stuff?" Johnson asked, peering down at a spread of bagels, lox and cream cheese.

"What do you mean?" I asked. "This is like the Jewish National Dish. You can't come to the Catskills without eating bagels and lox."

"Look, Lipsen," he said, jabbing a finger at me, "if somebody here wants to call me an anti-Semite [he pronounced it anti-se-MITT] 'cause I won't eat this funny-lookin' crap, I'll take a chance on it. Christ, that stuff'll give me cramps."

"Okay, okay, I just thought I'd surprise you."

"Why don't you surprise me with just some eggs and grits?" he asked, and then turned away to chat with some of his aides.

139

Eggs and grits in the Catskill Mountains are about as plentiful as outhouses on Park Avenue. Where the hell would I get grits at the Nevele Country Club?

"The closest we come," Slutsky said, "is Cream of Wheat."

I looked over the cereal, nodded and said, "Okay. But make it lumpy. Maybe he won't know the difference."

He knew. "This may be a helluva nice place," he told me later, "but they sure got lousy grits."

The real crisis came later in the day when a call came from Marty Underwood at the White House. When Johnson hung up he called me to him and was furious.

"I thought I gave you explicit instructions that nobody's reservation was to be canceled," he fumed.

"Nobody's was," I said. "At least, that's what Slutsky said."

"Slutsky, smutsky," Johnson said. "A guy named Sugarman called the White House in Washington and complained he had to cancel his honeymoon trip because of my visit here. If he gives it to the press, I'll look like hell."

"Let me look into it," I said. "I'm sure there's some mistake."

"I'm sure there is, too," he said. "And it looks like it's yours."

I practically tackled Slutsky when I saw him a few moments later walking in the lobby. I told him what had happened. We went over his records and, sure enough, a Mr. Sugarman from Chicago had been canceled.

"But his reservation was only tentative," Slutsky maintained. "And I canceled him before he could send a deposit."

I grabbed the reservation card and immediately placed a call to Sugarman. An elderly-sounding man answered, and I put Slutsky on the phone. I listened on an extension.

"Is Mr. Sugarman there?" he asked.

"This is Sugarman," the man answered.

"I mean, is there another Mr. Sugarman, a young man who made honeymoon reservations at the Nevele?"

"That's me," he said. "The very same."

Slutsky hesitated. "I'm calling on behalf of the President," he said.

"President who?"

"President Johnson."

"Oh," he said, "*that* President."

"Yes, Mr. Sugarman. He's very upset that your reservation was canceled here to make room for his party. But I want to assure you"—I looked hard at Slutsky—"that as soon as arrangements can be made, you and your bride will be guests of the hotel for an entire week."

Slutsky clapped his hand to his head like he had been shot between the eyes.

"That's very nice," Sugarman said. "I'm sure Mrs. Sugarman will love it like my previous wife."

"What's that again?" Slutsky asked.

"I always go to the Nevele," he said, "on each honeymoon."

I could barely contain myself when Slutsky hung up. Some young honeymooner, that Sugarman! When I reported back to the President, he was both relieved and amused.

"That must be some old stud," Johnson said. "How the hell you suppose he does it?"

"Bagels and lox," I deadpanned.

We collapsed in laughter.

Our next run-in didn't give Johnson any laughs. It was in Detroit, where I had helped put together a crowd of about 40,000 people. But the previous night, Johnson had made a trip to Wichita, substituting at the last minute for Humphrey. My brother, Zel, had advanced that trip since the plan was for a Humphrey appearance. Zel had called me in a panic the day before the rally, minutes after he learned the President would make the appearance instead.

"What the hell do I do with all the Humphrey signs?" he asked.

"Just change them, Zel. Have people write in Johnson above Humphrey's name, or where you've got HHH put on LBJ, too. Just be sure to put the President's name ahead of Hubert's."

His people worked through the night and most of the next day, but they made the changes. And a reported 65,000 people turned out. When Johnson got to Detroit and surveyed the crowd, he turned to me before going to the lectern and whispered: "It looks like I've got the wrong Lipsen working for me."

He might have been kidding then, but later, when he had finished his speech, he wasn't.

"How was it?" he asked Jack Valenti, one of his top aides and closest friends.

"You had them eating out of your hands," Valenti said.

"Chuck?" he asked, turning his satisfied smile on me.

"It stank," I said without hesitating. "You should've spoke twenty, thirty minutes at the outside and you went for an hour and a half. Boring, boring, boring."

"I see." He scowled.

That's all he said. But when the limousines picked us up to transport us to the airport, I somehow found myself without a seat. "Grab a cab," Johnson snapped from his car window.

There was no question I had been assigned to the back of the bus. About the only thing I had going for me then was that the Secret Service, which usually abhorred political advance men, had taken a shine to me. A friendly Secret Service guy could make an advance man's life considerably easier. If they didn't like you, which was the rule rather than the exception, they could and would veto nearly any idea you had for the President to mingle with a crowd, *shmoos* with political leaders or big contributors after a speech, or take a highly publicized and therefore crowded motor tour through a town.

But one of the top Secret Service men on the Johnson campaign, Andy Berger, liked me. The turning point had come just before Johnson's Detroit speech. I had persuaded Andy to join me for a couple of drinks. While we were chatting in a local bistro, Andy suddenly said, "Let's go someplace else."

I shrugged and agreed. At the next joint, Andy started acting jumpy again.

"What's wrong?" I asked.

"Turn around slow, but those two gorillas back against the wall are following us."

I felt like James Bond.

"Who are they?" I asked.

"FBI," he said casually. "They've been on my tail ever since Dallas. They want to get something on me."

Andy then told me what had transpired at Parkland Hospital in Dallas on the day President Kennedy was shot. Andy was assigned to a corridor leading to the emergency room in which the

President lay dead or dying. Suddenly, he said, a beefy man came rushing up the corridor and tried to get through to the emergency room.

"I've gotta get through," he said breathlessly. "I've gotta find out what's going on and report back to Washington."

"Nobody gets through," Andy said menacingly.

"I'm FBI," the man said officiously, and started reaching inside his coat, presumably for credentials.

"But I thought he was going for a gun," Andy told me. "I should have known better, but, Jesus, after what we had just been through, can you blame me for being jumpy?"

In any event, Berger grabbed the guy's arm, leaped forward and coldcocked him with a right cross to the jaw.

"I was embarrassed as hell," Andy told me, "and I apologized. But from that day, the FBI had it in for me."

"You mean to tell me that the FBI has got a couple of guys going around trying to get something on you?"

"You bet your ass," he said evenly. "They'd like nothing better than to find me with a babe or drunk the night before a presidential visit."

"Jesus," I said. "Is that the way Hoover spends money to fight crime?"

"Mine is not to reason why," Berger said. Then he loudly called over the waitress. "I'll have another Coke," he said. The waitress scratched her head, but did as she was told.

Then I got up and ambled toward the door, close to which the two men Berger suspected of being FBI agents were seated. As I approached, I pretended to trip into the table. As one of the men leaned forward to catch me to prevent me from falling, I spotted the outlines of a shoulder holster. He must have seen my eyes widen.

"We've got no quarrel with you, Lipsen," one of the men said, apparently unconcerned with my reaction to them knowing my name. "Our quarrel's with Andy Berger."

"You guys listen to me," I said bravely, knowing now they weren't hoods. "You get the hell out of here and leave us alone."

"This comes straight from the Director," the man said, referring to J. Edgar Hoover.

"I don't give a shit if it comes from God," I said. "You guys blow, or I report this directly to the President when he gets here. Then you'll all have hell to pay."

Whether they took my threat seriously or simply decided that discretion would be the better part of valor, they left immediately and without another word.

"Lipsen," Berger said admiringly when I returned to the table, "I've got to hand it to you. All the other advance men I've been hooked up with wouldn't have dared to open their mouths to the FBI." He called the waitress back.

"What the hell am I doing with this Coke?" he demanded. "Bring me a scotch on the rocks."

From that moment, I became fast friends with Berger and other Secret Service men with whom I traveled. Whatever I proposed as part of the President's program, they wouldn't tell me it couldn't be done. Instead, they said, okay, let's see if we can work this out. It made for relaxed, bigger, more successful appearances which the President appreciated and chalked up to some special expertise he assumed I had. It got so that when he planned an appearance in which he had particular interest, he'd tell me or other advance men assigned to the trip, "Now, I want to have one of those Cecil B. De Lipsen specials on this one."

But the Secret Service men liked to play little jokes on their friends. I had a particularly tricky assignment in Morgantown, West Virginia, in which the local steelworkers had been planning a strike and, when they heard Johnson was coming to town, they determined to turn out in force and heckle the President to dramatize their demands.

It took almost an entire day to persuade the union leadership that their beef wasn't with Johnson but with the steel companies. If they turned out in force with pro-Johnson signs and wouldn't heckle, I promised them the President would recognize their plight during his speech and openly side with their demands. It worked, and Johnson agreed to it.

But there was yet another problem. Both West Virginia senators, Jennings Randolph and Robert Byrd, wanted to introduce Johnson at the rally. It was a question of prestige and home-state publicity. "You work it out" were the only instructions I got from Washington.

I felt like King Solomon trying to figure out how to slice my President in half to please both senators. Finally, I hit on an idea. If I could get Johnson to call Byrd, who was then in Charleston, and invite him back to Washington so he could personally accompany the President on his trip to West Virginia, then I could give Randolph the honor of introducing Johnson without hurting Byrd's feelings. Johnson went for it and Byrd drove his own car back to the capital to board *Air Force One*. There were plenty of cameras and reporters on hand both at the airport (to watch Johnson descend arm in arm with Byrd from the presidential plane) and at the rally (to see Johnson give Randolph a bear hug after the introduction). It made everybody happy.

Needless to say, I was weary when I returned to the Holiday Inn after the President's departure. A new advance man and a relief team of Secret Service agents had been assigned to the next leg of the Johnson campaign, so I was looking forward to a good night's sleep.

I had a few belts with some agent friends and, as I was preparing to say good night, one of them said casually:

"By the way, Chuck, here's your room key. You're assigned in with John Chips tonight." The others could barely contain their amusement. I found out why later.

I knew Chips (who most recently was assigned to the Jimmy Carter campaign) only slightly. He seemed, like most of the Secret Service men, to be a bright, sharp guy. What I didn't know was that Chips, perhaps because of a deviated septum, was among the world's soundest sleepers—and loudest snorers. Chips snored so loudly that he couldn't hear a wake-up call or an alarm clock. One agent always kept an extra key to Chips's room so he could enter in the mornings and physically shake him awake. And Chips was the only agent allowed to have a hotel room to himself. No one would sleep with him. Actually, no one *could* sleep with him.

After the 1960 election of John Kennedy, Chips was assigned to the Kennedy compound in Hyannis Port. One night, seven of his colleagues carried the sleeping Chips, bed and all, to the front lawn. Neither the movement nor the cold, night air disturbed him—but next morning, some of Kennedy's neighbors complained about the loud, strange noises they heard in the night. It was Chips snoring. When Chips had married, some of his buddies presented his bride with a pair of Mickey Mouse earmuffs.

When I walked into the motel room where Chips already was asleep, I couldn't believe my ears. The sound varied from a constant roar like Niagara Falls to a sudden burst of noise like a Concorde SST taking off. There was no respite. I tossed and turned for an hour, pulled the covers over my head, buried my face ears-deep in the pillow. I stuffed corners of my socks into my ears. Nothing helped. I pulled on my pants, threw on a robe and walked around the motel for about a half-hour, thinking that might tire me enough to drop off. It didn't. At last, the idea hit me.

Next morning at breakfast, I walked jauntily into the dining room, freshly showered and shaved, and bounced into a seat to join several of the agents.

They looked at me closely. I was bright-eyed and bushy-tailed, hardly the picture of a man who had just spent a sleepless night in the same room with what compared to a brace of jackhammers.

"You sleep okay?" one of them asked offhandedly.

"Like a baby," I said happily. "Best night's sleep I've had in years."

They couldn't stand it any more. "Okay, Lipsen," said one, "come clean. How the hell did you sleep with John Chips in the same room? Did you get another room or something?"

"Hell, no," I said. "I stayed right where you put me. In fact, it was Chips who got another room."

"How'd you manage that?"

"It was easy," I explained. "To tell you the truth, I was pretty pissed off at you guys for a while. I tried everything to drown that son of a bitch out. Then I remembered a trick my wife used when I got to snoring too loudly. I walked over to his bed, leaned over, and I blew in his ear."

"You what?"

"Blew in his ear. He rolled over and cracked his eyes open. 'Who are you?' he asked me. 'I'm Lipsen,' I said. 'You remember. The Johnson advance man. I'm your roomie tonight.' Then I leaned over and patted him on the cheek and said, 'Good night, sweetie.' Then I hopped into bed. A second later, the poor bastard sat bolt upright and I'm pretty sure he just stared at me for ten minutes wondering what the hell I might do next. He must have decided not to wait around to find out, 'cause he grabbed his overnight bag and got the hell out of there."

We all joked about the incident for months, but I don't think John Chips ever had another roommate after that.

Still, there weren't many nights in which I could enjoy a peaceful sleep. Johnson was a compulsive campaigner who never wasted a minute. And when he worked, he expected his aides to work twice as hard. Once, after a successful rally I had put together in Jeffersonville, Indiana, Johnson grabbed my arm and instructed me to follow him as he made his way up the street shaking hands, nodding benignly and squeezing out that pursed, almost pained grin of his.

We walked into the post office building, where he continued waving and pressing flesh until he was shown into the postmaster's office. He waved me in behind him.

"Okay," he said, "brief me on my next stop."

"You want to sit down?" I asked as I pulled out my note pad.

"Not here," he said. "There." With that, he marched to the private toilet, pulled down his trousers and sat upon the seat.

"I'll wait here," I said modestly.

"I don't have time," he instructed. "Come on in here."

There is something about chatting with a President who is sitting on the pot that tends to strip away the regality of the office. Whatever else might be said about the growth and dangers of the imperial presidency, the exigencies of politics are a great equalizer of men.

But more than long hours drained me on the Johnson campaign. The almost constant emotional tension he generated among his staff could be more sapping than three days without sleep.

Once, I was dropped off at Burlington, Vermont, by a staff jet with instructions from Jack Valenti to make arrangements for a quick airport stop. A stand-up microphone would be sufficient, he had said.

By the time Johnson showed up, the locals and I had whipped up a crowd of about 50,000. As he descended from the plane with Johnson, Valenti began chastising me for what he called inadequate preparations. Johnson, who overheard, grew dark.

"How the hell can I talk to these people without a podium?" he asked. "Nobody'll see or hear me."

Fortunately, I had planned for such an eventuality and, at that moment, a large mobile podium was being rolled into place complete with sophisticated sound gear. The President's mood lightened as he mounted the steps to shrieks of support.

"You didn't have to do that," I snarled at Valenti. "Bad-mouthing me in front of the Boss. First off, you know goddam well you told me all we needed was a stand-up mike."

"I said nothing of the sort," Valenti said.

"The hell you didn't," chirped George Reedy, the President's press secretary. "I heard you."

"That's sure as hell the truth," added Mac Kilduff, an assistant press secretary.

Valenti looked at us and then allowed as how he was sorry.

"It's not enough to tell me you're sorry," I said. "Make damn sure *he* knows about it," I added, gesturing at Johnson.

I don't know if Jack or anyone else ever told Johnson that I hadn't screwed up, after all, at Burlington. But he kept me in his entourage, nonetheless. But that kind of internecine aggravation was exacerbated by Janice's schedule. I would no sooner get home from a tiring trip when she would be off on one of her own for the Young Citizens group. In fact, while I was at the Ho-Hum Motel, of all place names, following the Burlington flare-up, I received an SOS from Jan, who was preparing a Johnson barbecue in Newark.

While meeting with local political leaders, Jan had been introduced to the Big Man, Mayor Hugh Addonizio. We both knew Addonizio slightly. Until he became mayor of Newark in 1962, he had been a congressman for twelve years. But neither of us knew Addonizio well enough to prepare Jan for that encounter.

"He just laid it on the line," Jan told me. "He said he expected to get half the take from the barbecue for the local political organization or there'd be no barbecue for Johnson or anyone else in his town. Those were his exact words."

"Jesus," I breathed. "Can't you tell him to do a special favor for the President? I'll make sure LBJ does a real smoke job on him."

"I tried that," Jan sighed. "He wants money, not smoke."

"Will you have to cancel?"

"I don't know what to do. That's why I called you."

"Okay," I said. "Sit tight and I'll get back to you."

I put in a call to Paul Hall of the Seafarers Union, a tough old bird who was also an old friend. He turned me over to one of his aides, to whom I explained the situation.

"All right," he said, "I'll tell you what we do. You tell Jan to go ahead. There's nothing Addonizio can do directly to stop a presidential function. But . . ." His voice took on an ominous inflection.

"But what?" I asked.

"These are tough cookies she's playing with up there," he said. "They can't stop the function, once it's set. But they could try to stop her."

"What the hell does that mean?"

"Just what it sounds like."

"Good God," I said, "I've got to get her the hell out of there!"

"No, let her go ahead. I'll take care of her."

"Listen, baby, don't fuck up," I said. "This is my wife we're talking about."

"Leave it to me."

I got back to Jan and told her that Paul's boys were taking care of things. I told her there was nothing to worry about. A half-hour later, the phone rang in my room at the Ho-Hum. It was Jan, a woman who I had never seen fazed by childbirth, politics, moves across the country or anything. But this time, for the first time in my life, I could tell she was scared as hell.

149

"There are these two gorillas outside my door," she whispered. "And I mean they're gorillas."

"What do they want?"

"I don't know. They knocked on the door and when I answered, they just said they would hang around, that I shouldn't mind them."

I thought a moment. "Jan," I said, "just hang on a few minutes. Don't open the door for anyone. I'll run down the hall to a pay phone and call the Seafarers."

I was short of change, so I put the call on my government credit card. Hell, I thought, the taxpayers wouldn't mind. Besides, this was an emergency. He came right on the line and explained the whole thing. I raced back to Jan.

"Everything's all right," I said. "Those are Paul's guys. They're your bodyguards while you're in Newark, just in case Addonizio tries anything funny."

"These guys look mean, Chuck," she said.

"They are," I answered. "But they're on your side. Just don't worry."

The barbecue came off and even Addonizio showed up. But Jan wisely skipped town immediately after the event, and neither of us have been back to Newark since, even though Addonizio has since gone to jail for extortion.

Not all Jan's barbecues were that exciting. One, planned for Minnesota, seemed so dull, in fact, that she and Esther wanted to cancel it themselves. Even though Minnesota was the home state of the vice-presidential candidate, Senator Humphrey, the incumbent governor, Karl Rolvaag, was a political amateur. His "organization," such as it was, seemed unable to sell enough tickets to make the event worthwhile.

But a young Humphrey protégé named Walter (Fritz) Mondale offered to take over the effort. He was the state's attorney general and he was willing to embarrass the governor to make the barbecue a success. Else, Humphrey would be embarrassed.

Both Esther and Jan were impressed with him—and with his ability to generate a record crowd for the barbecue. They were so impressed that they phoned me and urged me to enlist Johnson's support to have Mondale appointed to replace Humphrey in the Senate after the expected Johnson-Humphrey landslide in November.

Rolvaag had intended to resign as governor and have his successor appoint him to the Senate for Humphrey's seat. But Esther and Jan were convinced that Rolvaag would be defeated easily in the next general election. Mondale, they thought, had the ability and the popularity to retain the seat for the Democrats.

Dutifully, I called on Johnson, even though I had wanted to plump for Representative John Blatnick for the seat.

"I don't know the first thing about Mondale, Mr. President," I admitted, "but Esther and Jan think he's first rate. Better than Rolvaag, in any case, and better able to keep the seat. Maybe you should ask Hubert . . ."

"That's not necessary," he said, and I was sure he already had. "If Esther and Jan say he's good, that's enough for me."

He was at it again, I knew. Pretending he was taking our advice when, in fact, he probably already knew whether or not Mondale had a birthmark on his fanny.

But he picked up the phone and, with me across the desk, placed a call to Rolvaag and gave him a half-hour snow job. "Great governor . . . brilliant record . . . farsighted programs . . ." . . . and then the crusher—". . . shrewd politician."

Johnson said that he already guessed that Rolvaag would name Mondale to Humphrey's seat. It would be a "master stroke of politics," he said, "to assure the party could keep the seat." And, Johnson added, "I won't forget it. I'll take good care of any man who goes the extra mile for the party."

Mondale got the job, kept it, and, of course, became vice-president. Minnesotans seemed to have a lock on that job, as far as Democrats were concerned.

Things quieted down for me after Johnson's huge election victory, though he still called on me to advance portions of his major trips. Some of them, however, were nerve-racking—what I called "two-shirt trips" because I would sweat so heavily from the tension, I'd have to change my shirt twice in the same day.

One of those was in July 1968, when Johnson went to El Salvador for a Central American economic conference. When the conference was over, Johnson planned to accompany each Central American President to the airport of his capital. My assignment, with Bob Hardesty, was to advance the stop Johnson would make in Managua with President Samoza.

We were understandably nervous. Bobby Kennedy had been killed the month before by Sirhan Sirhan and Secret Service Agent Ron Pontius was especially pressured by the knowledge that several thousand Arabs lived in Nicaragua. An Israeli colonel had telephoned me saying that many of the Arabs were anti-Israel fanatics. The word was that Sirhan had shot Kennedy to protest the senator's views toward the Middle East. Might not some nut try to do the same to Johnson when he alighted from the airplane or while he stood next to Samoza? (Pontius, incidentally, was to experience a near tragedy first-hand some years later. It was he who draped his body over President Ford's and shoved the President into his limousine when Sara Jane Moore fired an errant shot in their direction.)

The three of us met with Nicaragua's military chief to discuss the situation.

"I don't know that there is much we can do," the Nicaraguan said in accented English. "Of course," he added, "we can simply round up all the Arabs in the city and detain them until your President has departed."

"I don't think we can allow that," Hardesty said. But I kicked him under the table and interjected, "That sounds fine, sir, just fine." Pontius nodded his agreement.

Later, Hardesty told me I was crazy. "We can't approve that kind of thing, Chuck," he said. "You just don't go around arresting people for no reason."

"Not in our country, you don't," I agreed. "But this isn't the United States. I sure as hell hate dictatorships, but there are times when they are damned expedient."

Still, when we were at the airport standing near Johnson, the back of my neck tingled with the expectation of being struck by a rifle bullet at any moment. I was dripping by the time Johnson took off for his next stop.

A few days later, my father telephoned me in Washington. He had seen films of Johnson's Managua stop.

"I saw when the President was talking with you, you weren't

looking on him. That's very bad manners, you should know," he said accusingly.

"Dad, I was looking around for snipers. That was more important than being polite."

"Snipers?" he said. "And what do you do if you see one?"

"You're supposed to throw yourself on the President," I said.

"And would you?"

"I'd probably run the other way."

He paused. "Okay. Polite you're not. Smart, you are."

But Johnson tried to see to it that, once in a while, we had some fun trips. In October 1966 he had decided that I had qualified for one.

Johnson's usual obsession for secrecy kept me from knowing what it was about until it was almost time to depart. Until then, all I knew was I had to prepare to go overseas and that it was important enough for me to miss being with my wife for our October 12 anniversary party.

"I can't tell you what's happening," White House aide Leonard Marks told me a few hours before we boarded *Air Force Two* to follow the President, "but, because you've handled a lot of shit details in the past, the Boss thinks you're entitled to a piece of cake."

Johnson was embarking on a major trip that would take him to Australia and to Vietnam. En route, he would be refueling in Samoa. And I was being assigned the advance work for that Pacific paradise—and I would have more than two weeks to do a job that would probably take about two hours.

The party mood took hold while we were flying to Hawaii, where we would drop off Joe Laitin and Marcia Maddox, who would advance that leg of the trip. I was having such a good time that Juanita Roberts, one of LBJ's top personal secretaries, assigned me to a bunk behind the cockpit to keep me out of the clutches of a beautiful young secretary (or vice versa). Juanita and my wife were good friends. "If you're gonna fool around," she chastised, "it's not gonna be with me around or on your anniversary."

When I got to Samoa, a pearl of an island with 26,000 natives, I checked in with Governor Rex Lee. We made arrangements for

153

Johnson's arrival, for the dedication of the new Lady Bird Johnson School, and for an educational television broadcast. The next day, I went native.

I donned sandals and the traditional native sarong called a *lava-lava*. I lay on the beach drinking beer and the potent local concoction called *kava-kava*. Wearing my *lava-lava* and drinking *kava-kava*, I ogled the local damsels in their revealing wraparounds called *poulatasis*. Except for a trip to Rainmaker Mountain and chatting with the chiefs (separated into high chiefs and talking chiefs, though I never was sure of the distinction), the rest of the two weeks was a blur. I vaguely recall, however, that I came to know and love the Samoans.

I became so deeply engrossed in absorbing native culture (along with *kava-kava*) that I somehow never responded to a couple of urgent calls from Washington to check on the arrangements. Johnson assistants Bill Moyers and Liz Carpenter became concerned enough to send an SOS to Laitin and Maddox in Honolulu and order them to hop the next plane to Samoa (there were four each week) and find out what happened to me.

One of their concerns, of course, was that there be a mighty welcome for the President when his plane put in. They needn't have worried about that. Anytime an eagle landed in Samoa, the natives found it cause for great excitement. The arrival of a plane was practically a national holiday rivaling anything that Fletcher Christian might have seen when the *Bounty* anchored off Tahiti.

So it was that when the plane carrying Laitin and Maddox landed in Samoa, a huge crowd surrounded the silver bird.

As the nearsighted Ms. Maddox recalls, she came down the steps of the plane without her glasses and everything looked like a colorful blur. Squinting, she remembers, she saw a faintly familiar figure near the ramp. Naked from the waist up except for a Caesar-like garland of flowers crowning his head, and garbed in a *lava-lava*, he had an arm draped around the waist of a local lovely wearing her *poulatasi*.

She approached slowly and then ventured, "Chuck? Is that you?"

It was, and I welcomed my two Washington friends to the joys of Samoa for the next several hours. On their departure, I wanted to assure them that everything was ready for Johnson's arrival. Hundreds of natives lined up to watch the takeoff.

"Now, here's how it'll be," I said. "The cameras'll be over there and the chiefs and Governor Lee will be around the ramp. Just as the President boards and turns to wave, the natives'll wave good-by. Watch. This'll kill you."

I turned and shouted, "Now, everybody, wave good-by!"

With that, all the men in the crowd pulled off their *lava-lavas* and started waving them frantically. As was the custom, they wore nothing underneath. They were stark naked. Laitin and Maddox blanched.

"Won't the President like that?" I deadpanned. "I thought it would look great on TV."

Then I doubled with laughter, and when they realized I would use greater discretion for Johnson's departure, they laughed, too.

Johnson was in high spirits when he arrived. He wanted to try some *kava-kava* but the Secret Service vetoed the idea. "I want to come back here, Lipsen," he said, "in about nine months—and find out how much of a population explosion you caused."

As it turned out, Johnson returned about a year later. Prime Minister Harold Holt of Australia had drowned in a tragic accident and Johnson, who was making another Far Eastern tour in December of 1967, decided personally to attend the funeral. Again I was sent to Samoa.

This time it was raining when the President arrived. He was in a bitchy mood, apparently nursing a cold, and he decided to stay on board during the refueling stop. But I sent word to the plane insisting he come down, if only to please the thousands who had waited patiently in the rain to cheer his arrival.

He consented, but as he descended, I could see he was in one of his dark moods. He perfunctorily greeted the governor and the chiefs but grew interested when a group of twenty beautiful native children, dressed in impeccably white *lava-lavas* and *poulatasis* began singing a Christmas carol I had taught them.

"What the hell is that?"

"They're singing for you," I said. "I taught them a song."

"I didn't think you knew any Christmas carols," he said.

"I wrote this one. Listen closely."

The kids did beautifully, especially enunciating the principal lyric:

God rest ye, merry LBJ, Let nothing you dismay,
Remember, even Jesus Christ was not loved ev'ry day . . .

Johnson loved it. "Who are these kids?" he asked.

"Remember what you said last time you were here?" I responded. "About me and the population explosion? Well, there's the result," I said, gesturing at the line of kids.

"Good God," he sighed. "If I send you back here again, we'll have enough people for a fifty-first state."

But then the cares of Vietnam again clouded his face. "I got to go," Johnson said anxiously. He thanked me for the pleasant respite in what he said would be a difficult and disheartening trip.

Though Johnson ended his presidency with Vietnam draped around his neck like an albatross, one which would forever stain his place in history, no one could ever say that the decisions he made, however ill-advised, were made lightly or without etching deep scars into his soul.

He would wake nights from a sleep troubled by visions of young men being sent to their deaths. He would pace in the early hours or impulsively grab a telephone to discuss again and again a decision he had just made putting even more Americans in jeopardy.

One such night in February of 1968, he telephoned the commanding general of the 82nd Airborne Division at Fort Bragg, North Carolina, saying he would come next day to meet with and speak to some troops bound for duty in Vietnam. That was the occasion for one of the last advance trips I ever made for Johnson.

I was awakened during the night by a phone call from Jim Jones, a White House aide who, more recently, has been a congressman from Oklahoma.

Jones told me to hop a plane at Andrews Air Force Base near Washington first thing in the morning and set up a trip the President was making to see some troops. I was to meet Major General Richard Seitz and Brigadier General Donald Blackburn, the division's commanders (Blackburn was the man who later led the brave but vain raid to free American POWs from Son Tay, a site where it had been believed they were interned by the North Vietnamese).

When I hit the ground, I had barely an hour to put the thing together. I arranged for a flat-bed truck and sound equipment from which Johnson would tell the troops how proud he was of the sacrifices they were about to make for their country. I planned a twenty-minute visit by the President to the nearby infirmary, where he could meet the recently returned wounded.

Then it came time to get a battalion or two in battle dress to meet their Commander-in-Chief. A battalion scheduled to leave next day seemed the likeliest, but a wizened career sergeant took me to meet some of the men at a beer club, where, predictably, they were getting tanked up before departing the country and, quite possibly, the world.

"You don't want these guys, do you?" he asked.

"Hell, no," I said. "See if you can get some other guys."

Dutifully, the sergeant, after checking with the generals, rounded up a couple of battalions that would be leaving for Vietnam in a week or two. Briefly, it crossed my mind that Johnson might be angry, that he wanted to see and speak to young soldiers who were shipping out almost immediately. But then I decided it didn't matter that much; the poor bastards would be going soon enough.

Almost as soon as the President touched down, I realized it wouldn't matter at all. Johnson had taken pains to make sure a healthy segment of the press was along for the ride. It suddenly dawned on me that the 1968 New Hampshire primary was around the corner and that Senator Eugene McCarthy of Minnesota was gaining dangerously in the polls. Johnson had staged a media event that he thought might take some of the sting out of Vietnam in time for the voting. He wouldn't care if the soldiers out there were trained baboons. In fact, it had been a White House aide who reminded me before my departure to "make sure they have some salt and pepper up front"—White House terminology meaning it wanted the front ranks noticeably dotted with Negroes. That, too, was less racial concern, I realized, and more for public consumption.

Johnson threw a curve after he had talked to the troops and walked among their ranks shaking hands. He wanted to see the men taking off so he could wish them farewell.

That made me nervous. These guys weren't leaving for a while, yet I didn't want to cross Johnson. Whether he wanted to bid them adieu for sentiment or merely to provide still more good pictures and film footage, I didn't know. But I thought discretion was warranted. I slipped over to a captain who was an aide to General Seitz and told him what the President wanted.

"It'll take a few minutes, sir," he said. "But I think we can arrange to roll up a plane."

I told Johnson that preparations were being completed, so why didn't he come along to the infirmary and then return to the strip to say good-by? He agreed.

By the time we got back, a transport had been rolled up and the men dutifully boarded while Johnson stood there and shook each man's hand.

The plane began taxiing and I herded Johnson back toward *Air Force One.* "Damn fine boys," he said, and I thought his eyes were glistening.

I don't think that transport ever took off. It probably taxied around for a few minutes and then let out its passengers. Johnson got his publicity, but it didn't seem to help much in New Hampshire. A few weeks later, he decided to pull out of the race in 1968 while simultaneously announcing some new peace initiatives.

On one hand, it was a crass piece of media manipulation that most incumbent Presidents are expert at. But on the other, Johnson was, at that moment, in the throes of trying to decide whether to beef up his Vietnamese forces by yet another 200,000 men or find some way out of the morass he had placed himself and his country into. Unknown to any of us, of course, was that he was also wrestling with the enormously heavy decision of whether to withdraw from the re-election campaign.

It was almost impossible to separate Johnson the Politician

from Johnson the Man. They were inextricably bound. He might have been genuinely moved at meeting men bound for a dirty war. But he sure as hell wanted his picture made doing it.

Rightly or wrongly, I had adopted, perhaps through proximity, those same instinctive principles. I don't think a politician or a lobbyist is shorn of emotion. But he is capable of sidetracking or channeling that emotion to suit his ends. And the extent to which I had depended on Johnson for my political growth and training flooded my mind five years after that day in Fort Bragg.

Johnson had died in Texas and had been flown to Washington to lie in state in the rotunda of the Capitol. One of Johnson's aides called me and said that Mrs. Johnson would like me to join the honor guard at his coffin for an hour. I started to go immediately but Janice insisted I change from a checked suit into a somber dark one. It almost made me late.

I got there in time to join three others standing silently by the catafalque between one and two in the morning. Despite the hour, people streamed through. Not in the numbers they had when John Kennedy had lain there, but a sufficient number to help us all remember the enormous impact the man had on crucial domestic issues that we hoped would live longer than the memory of Vietnam.

Suddenly, I saw a woman carrying a small boy in her arms, a child no more than three years old. As they circled behind me, I could hear a man next to her ask why she had brought the baby out in the middle of the night.

"I couldn't get here sooner," she said, "and I wanted to be able to tell my son that he had paid his respects to President Johnson. He helped a lot of us poor."

With that, a marine tapped my shoulder and said it was time for the next group of honor guards. It was none too soon. I walked to a corner off the rotunda and I cried for my friend; I cried for what history would surely say of him because of Vietnam though I knew how hard he had tried and how desperately he had wanted to be remembered for his Great Society. And I cried for myself; I cried for all those crazy, tense, exciting days in which I had been Cecil B. De Lipsen—and I knew they would be no more.

159

13

GET SMART

There is a tendency among many lobbyists to develop "eye" trouble. Except it's spelled "I"—"I was the one who put over the vote," "I wrote that great speech for Senator Cleghorn"—I did this, I did that.

It's all part of the smart-aleck syndrome that rarely affects a person who is in public life and who gets the credit and the attention that usually accrues to those elected to office.

But for those who operate in their shadow, whether as congressional aides or lobbyists, the frustration of doing much of the work and never getting the credit for it can become palpable. The result is that many of us start shooting off our mouths about our achievements, real and imagined, and violate the first commandment of the good political assistant coined during his first term by President Franklin Roosevelt: "The ideal political aide," FDR told an aide who had been upstaging the President with recent statements to the press, "is a man who has a passion for anonymity."

Most of the time, I had the prudence, if not the passion, to remain safely backstage. Once in a while, against my better judgment, I emerged long enough to let people know that I was the real force behind certain legislative goals. I got away with it most of the time.

The first time was when I decided to play congressman myself. It happened shortly after the Senate debate over the proposed anti-ballistic missile program. I had been lobbying on behalf of the ABM for the AFL-CIO, which supported it on the grounds it would create thousands of new jobs. One day, however, when I called on Senator Schweiker of Pennsylvania, he ordered me to come into his office and sit down.

He proceeded to lecture me for half an hour on the foolhardiness of the ABM program. Not only would it cost too much, he said, but it would start a spiral of escalation of research and development between the United States and the Soviet Union. If we developed an anti-ballistic missile, they would develop a missile to knock out the anti-ballistic missile—an anti-anti-ballistic missile. Then we'd get an AAABM to counter the AABM they had to knock out our ABM, which was designed to foil their first barrage of missiles. And so on. Finally, he persuaded me that by the time we developed such a weapon it would be obsolete. There was little question the whole thing would create an enormous number of jobs. But he made it sound as if we'd wind up with the world resembling a bunch of kids playing in a sandbox filled with detonating caps.

That same day, I reported to George Meany that I could no longer lobby on behalf of the ABM. I expected him to explode, but he just puffed his cigar and said, "Okay. Get off it."

"I thought you'd want me to resign," I said.

"No," he said. "As long as you're with me ninety-five per cent, I can be flexible."

He ordered me off the job and that left me with virtually nothing to do for a few weeks while the ABM was the principal piece of business for AFL-CIO lobbyists.

That's when I hatched my notion to develop a bill of my own, to work on behalf of a cause *pro bono*, as it were. A friend of mine happened to mention to me one day the number of kids who were dying or becoming severely ill because they were getting hold of poisons or strong drugs in their own homes. He didn't know that he had hit an old sore nerve. I had never felt completely comfortable about my role, when working for the paint industry, in keeping a poison label off certain paints which, when they peeled and were ingested, could prove fatal. So I figured I had a chance to make up for it.

I drew up a bill called the poison prevention packaging law which would require manufacturers of drugs and medicines to devise bottle caps with special safety features making them next to impossible for children to open. I talked to a number of members in the House and Senate and many were enthusiastic. The trouble was they were so busy with currently major issues, few had time to do more than attach their names to it.

So I decided to try a special ploy to help make them aware of the bill. Though Shakespeare had asked, "What's in a name?" I remembered Harry Truman's old story that before you could train a mule, you had to thwack it over the nose with a two-by-four. "That way," he'd say, "you'll get its attention."

I went to Senator Ted Moss of Utah to win his agreement to sponsor the bill. Next I got the same approval from his distant cousin in the House, Representative John Moss of California. It is the custom in Congress to call a bill by the names of its chief Senate and House sponsors. So this became known as the Moss-Moss bill. The press had little humorous squibs about the bill's name which, in turn, prompted a few editorials saying that the name might be funny, but the purpose of the bill was deadly serious. The publicity, in turn, prompted the commerce committees in the two chambers to conduct hearings. The industry predictably objected to the proposal on grounds of cost—an estimated one-fourth cent per new cap. But no congressman would dare vote against a bill that might save one child's life for want of an extra quarter of a cent spent on a bottle of poison he might discover and use.

Still, there was the old problem of getting the bill scheduled for a vote. The Senate moved quickly but Harley Staggers of West Virginia, chairman of the House Commerce Committee, complained he could not get the bill placed on the House calendar for action.

I persuaded Staggers to try the strategy of bringing it up on Calendar Wednesday. Every Wednesday at the start of House proceedings, any member could call up a bill for placement on the House calendar as long as there was unanimous consent. The trick was to do it, if there was the least controversy, on a morning when the chamber might be virtually empty—and when known opponents to the measure were going to be absent. In this case, however, there was not concerted opposition. The only problem was that Staggers had not thought of it himself and thus, as is often the case with high-ranking elected officials, did not consider the measure particularly important. Nonetheless, he agreed to try—and the proposal sailed through unscathed and quickly became law.

Everything would have stopped there except for my big mouth. I couldn't help myself from spreading the word that I had been the power behind the whole thing—from drafting the bill to finding its sponsors to developing publicity for it to getting it on the House calendar. The result was that I suddenly encountered a perceptible chill from Staggers and the two Mosses. An aide to one of them took me aside in the Senate cafeteria to tell me the problem.

"You better apologize to those men," he advised. "My boss put it like this: 'If that SOB wants to lobby, let him stick to lobbying. If he wants to get votes, let him run for Congress. But until he does, tell him to keep his mouth shut and let the actors take the bows.'"

It was well taken. I apologized profusely to all concerned.

The next time I slipped may have been due less to forgetting the lesson I had learned than to the succession of Richard Nixon to the presidency. For one thing, Johnson's departure initially reduced my personal status as a key lobbyist. For another, with the GOP in power the influence of the labor movement was perceptibly decreased. Lastly, I disliked Richard Nixon politically, intellectually and viscerally. If I had any opportunity to make it known I was responsible for being a thorn in his side, I wouldn't miss it for the world.

So when the gargantuan battles involving Nixon's Supreme Court appointments of, first, Clement Haynsworth and, next, G. Harrold Carswell came along, I couldn't have been more eager to dive into them. I relished the chance to exercise once again whatever influence I could muster to persuade the Congress to my point of view. And I would be fighting Nixon, to boot.

I was assigned to work the Senate Republicans in the Haynsworth fight. My biggest personal coup came when Hugh Scott, who had been trying to remain neutral as long as he could, finally gave me a commitment to vote against Haynsworth. Though he didn't say so, Scott may have been repaying a debt from his campaign to become the Senate minority leader to replace Everett Dirksen. I had served as Scott's campaign manager in that successful effort. Now, having the Republican leader in the Senate on our side against the nominee of a Republican President virtually assured Haynsworth's defeat.

The bigger problem came with the Carswell nomination. At an AFL-CIO lobbying strategy session, where it had been decided to go after Carswell, I predicted we didn't have a snowball's chance in hell of winning. The Senate might defeat one Nixonian Supreme Court nominee, but not two. Besides, we didn't have an issue on Carswell like we did on Haynsworth, who had once failed to recuse himself in a decision involving a labor dispute of a company in which he had stock. He had supported the company decision and it carried the appearance of impropriety. Though Carswell got tagged with some racially vituperative statements from years before, he had since renounced those remarks. And to all appearances and initial professional reports, he was a competent judge.

What emerged, of course, was Carswell's obvious lack of judicial talent. A nice man, Carswell simply lacked the kind of legal credentials one would expect for a member of the Supreme Court. And when even one of his staunchest Senate supporters, Roman Hruska of Nebraska, could respond to Carswell's critics by only weakly suggesting that "mediocre" people deserved representation on the Supreme Court, we suddenly had a fighting chance.

This time, however, the Republicans were holding back. Scott, for one, said he couldn't go along with me this time. He had promised the President, he said, to stick with him. "But the bastard lied to me, Chuck," Scott said. "He told me the guy was clean and well recommended. And he turns out to be an old segregationist with a pea brain."

"If he lied to you," I said, "then you're not committed. That's the way it works."

"I know, I know," he sighed, puffing his pipe. "That's the way it *usually* is. But the minority leader can't kick his own President in the seat of the pants twice in a row."

Then he leaned toward me confidentially. "I'll tell you what I *will* do," he said. "I'll tell you a couple of people you just might want to spend some time with on this one. And if you do, you might just come out on top."

Scott proceeded to tick off the names of seven senators. If I could nail down four of them, he said, we should be able to beat Carswell.

I went to work promptly, concentrating on four considered sure bets by the other side. Two were Oregon's senators, the moderates Robert Packwood and Mark Hatfield. Their problem was twofold: they were Republicans who believed that when possible (which hadn't been too frequently) they should support their Republican Administration; and they believed that a President had the right to name his own man to the Supreme Court. As it turned out, they didn't need much convincing. They had been shocked by the mountain of evidence that Carswell was incompetent to sit on the Supreme Court. They gave me commitments within minutes of my having called on them.

Next came a Democrat, Tom Dodd of Connecticut. Dodd was considered a liberal on domestic matters, but he had been stung by his own Democratic congressional leadership in the flap over his use of campaign funds for personal purposes. He was formally reprimanded by the Senate and he was bitter. He was in no mood to join the Democratic pack in what was considered by many little more than an effort by one party to embarrass the leader of the opposition party.

"Senator," I appealed, "forget everything else for a minute.

165

Remember what this guy stood for on the racial issue. How does that strike you?"

"As despicable," he said.

"And, number two, remember you're a lawyer, a key member of the Senate Judiciary Committee. From that standpoint, how does Carswell measure up?"

"He doesn't," Dodd said.

"So? Need I say more?"

"No," he said promptly, "you don't. I'm in."

Lastly, there was Margaret Chase Smith of Maine. Mrs. Smith made it a rule never to announce her vote on a key issue in advance. She gave no pledges. She would listen politely to anyone's argument, thank them and dismiss them.

I gave her my Carswell pitch, emphasizing the likelihood that the issue could be decided by a single vote.

"I've always told you, Chuck," she said, "that I don't announce my votes. But on pain of death—yours, that is—I'll tell you on this one. I'm going to vote 'no.'"

I was elated. Those were the four I needed. I won over the other three waverers, too—Alan Bible, another Democrat, Charles Percy and Bill Saxbe—but that was gravy. The problem was that I couldn't contain my elation—not even when I ran into my old friend Ken Belieu, who was then working as one of Nixon's key lobbyists for the White House.

"How goes it?" he asked, attempting to be offhand. We both knew what he wanted.

"I got you," I said, allowing myself a satanic grin.

"Nuts," he replied.

"I got you, friend."

"Like who?"

"You know the waverers," I said. "Name some."

"Packwood," he said.

"He's okay."

"Hatfield."

"Him, too."

"Dodd."

"He's mine."

"Dodd, too?" he asked disbelievingly.

166

"Dodd, too."

He knew better than to ask about Maggie Smith. He assumed I wouldn't know about her, anyway.

"Now I'm worried," he said, looking worried. "I thought they were with me."

He walked off deep in thought while I nearly pranced to my car.

"You are stupid," Janice remonstrated that night when I told her of my encounter with Belieu. "Plain stupid."

"Aw, Jan," I puled, "I couldn't help myself. Ken's an old friend. He's a pro like I am."

"You sure didn't act like a pro. What do you suppose he's doing right now?"

"Screaming into his pillow?" I ventured.

"The heck he is," she replied. "What would you be doing if your opposite number walked up to you and gave you the names of the people you thought were with you but actually were going the other way?"

"I'd get back to every one of them and complain they'd broken their words to me."

"That's exactly what Ken is doing. You said you were a pro. You ought to start acting like one."

She was right, of course. In my eagerness to flaunt my victory over the opposition, to make sure that the other side knew that I, Charles Lipsen, had been responsible for pulling the key uncommitted votes to my side, I had been guilty of the worst kind of strategic error. It was no different from telling an opposing general in a war where, when and in what numbers your troops planned to launch a devastating attack.

I tossed and turned throughout the night, unable to sleep. I had blown it. I had succeeded in snatching defeat from the jaws of victory.

Next day, the excitement of the impending Carswell vote pumped enough adrenaline into me to wash away the fatigue of the sleepless night. I made a few discreet inquiries of staff members who worked for the waverers I had picked up earlier to ascertain if they were still on board or if Belieu had re-converted them.

"Did Ken Belieu get hold of your man last night?" I asked one.

"He did," the staffer answered, "and he was boiling."

"How come?"

"Ken thought the senator was pledged to the President and he heard a rumor that he got unhitched and had gone to your side."

"Well?"

"The senator's sticking with you. He never made any commitment to Ken."

"How did Ken get the idea he was committed the other way?" I asked.

"He had reached us late the other day and the senator had left. Ken talked to the legislative assistant, who told him he was sure the senator would go for Carswell."

That was the answer. Ken was a pro, all right, but he had made his own tactical mistake. He had gotten commitments, all right, but not from the members themselves. He had spoken to their staff people.

Key staff members are indispensable to the lobbyist. They do most of the work on issues and their recommendations to the member, based on research, talks with lobbyists and an understanding both of their boss's predilections and politics, are invariably followed.

But on a matter of conscience, congressmen will frequently throw politics to the wind. John Kennedy's *Profiles in Courage* amply demonstrated that as did the later House impeachment hearings of Richard Nixon. In the Carswell situation, each senator had to determine whether to support the tradition of allowing the President to select his own Supreme Court justice (especially in the wake of having just turned one down) or whether to reject Carswell because he plainly was not the caliber of man and lawyer for the job.

On a matter like that, you just couldn't confront a staff aide with your arguments. You had to see the senators themselves, to appeal directly not only to their minds but to their hearts. In the closing hours before the Senate vote, Belieu was too rushed to make direct appeals to every senator whose vote would prove crucial to the final outcome.

I heaved a sigh of relief and later took a seat in the Senate galleries with some colleagues. As the clerk called the roll, I played a little game. Before each response, I would quietly whisper "yea" or "nay" to my neighbor, demonstrating that I knew how each and every member would vote. When it came to Mrs. Smith, I leaned over and said, "No."

"No!" Mrs. Smith intoned, and there was a dramatic stir on the floor and among the onlookers.

"How did you know that?" my friend asked. "She never tells anyone how she'll vote."

"A lucky guess." I smiled.

Soon, it was over and we had won. Later in the afternoon, while we were back at the union offices celebrating, I got a phone call. It was Ken Belieu.

"It's always tough to lose a big one," Ken said, "but I wanted to congratulate you. You did a helluva job and you whipped us fair and square."

"You're some kind of guy," I said, genuinely touched. "Listen, I didn't mean to be a smart-ass yesterday."

"Hell, don't worry about that," he said. "It just showed me I had counted wrong. You're just damned lucky I wasn't able to pull those people back away from you. It would have been a different ball game."

It was a couple of weeks later that I learned Ken had called me only minutes after having been reprimanded by H. R. Haldeman in the presence of the President, even though Belieu had not predicted victory—only a close vote. To congratulate his opponent after having been dressed down in front of the President took more than a good loser. It took a good man.

I enjoyed the Carswell episode for more than the sense of victory it gave me. I enjoyed it because I really believed then and now that we kept from the Court a man unfit to join it. But it never should have come up in the first place. Had Haynsworth been confirmed, there would have been no Carswell incident—and, looking back, I believe we did Haynsworth an injustice by defeating his nomination. He continues to be a highly respected federal judge and a man of impeccable integrity. In retrospect, his "conflict of interest" was minor and excusable. And look where his defeat got us. For one thing, Nixon, after having lost two Supreme Court nominations in a row, was severely embarrassed—and I am certain the embarrassment hardened his notion that there were "enemies" all around him. It sharpened his resolve to beat those enemies at all costs—and there is no doubt in my mind that those setbacks led to some of the most glaring abuses of governmental power that came to be known as Watergate.

For another thing, it gave us William Rehnquist, a brilliant lawyer and a pleasant man, as the next member of the Supreme Court. To my mind, Rehnquist, despite his brilliance, will prove to be the most shockingly regressive, antediluvian justice in Supreme Court history. His rulings to date on individual rights and issues involving the First Amendment have demonstrated a frightening trend toward the repression of freedom. And, because of his youth, Rehnquist will be with us a long, long time.

If I had it to do over again, I would support Haynsworth for the Court. I believe it would have saved the country a great deal of grief from a petulant, vengeful Nixon, and from a Supreme Court justice with a mod haircut and a Stone Age mind.

14

BOODLE, BOOZE AND "THE EDGE OF NIGHT"

By the end of 1969, the Retail Clerks and I had had enough of one another. Johnson had been out of office for a year and Jim Suffridge had retired as president of the union. His replacement, Jay Housewright, had seemed vaguely uncomfortable with me, perhaps because of a report (wholly erroneous, it turned out) that I had secretly supported his opponent for the union presidency.

Meanwhile, I had been with the union long enough to receive a pension, I had made some successful investments and a friend of mine, a Washington lawyer, had lured me to join his firm with the promise of making a great deal of money.

He was right. In the next few months, I was raking in money at a pace that could put me over $100,000 in a year. I would arrange for building contractors to see the right people in the General Services Administration when they wanted a contract to put up a federal building. I arranged a merger deal for several contractors who wanted clearance from the antitrust division of the

Justice Department. And one client, a manufacturer of airplane equipment, took me on because someone in the Pentagon was trying to slip out of a contract with it in favor of a larger aerospace corporation which, to my mind, had a product no better than my client's yet was offering it for more money.

The problem was they had the pull and we didn't. I decided to get some action from congressmen. If I could get a few members to complain, I figured I could create enough of a problem to keep the Pentagon from changing horses in midair. I decided to call on my old friend Gaylord Nelson, senator from Wisconsin.

Nelson had been busy on some project of his own and he sent word he couldn't see me for a week. I didn't have that much time. Reaching back in my memory, I recalled that Nelson once had told me about a visit he received from Arnold Mayer, a key lobbyist for the Amalgamated Meat Cutters union. Arnold had been calling on senators regarding a poultry bill his union wanted passed. Within a minute, Nelson told Mayer that he was with him.

"Thank you, Senator," Nelson recalled Mayer telling him, "but I'd like to explain a few points of the bill to you."

"No need, Arnold," Nelson replied, "I'm with you."

But Arnold insisted on the ground the senator should be familiar with the intricacies of the measure. Arnold Mayer, without question, is among the most articulate, highly informed union lobbyists who has ever worked in Washington. But sometimes, his own intellect gets in the way of his basic lobbying. As soon as Nelson told Mayer that he was with him on the bill, Arnold should have tipped his hat, departed and spent his time with a waverer. But that's not Arnold. He sat down and, as Nelson remembers, he talked for the next solid hour about the ins and outs of the poultry bill. Finally, stifling a yawn, Nelson repeated he could be counted on to support the bill and Arnold finally took his leave.

Recalling Nelson telling the story, I confronted the senator's secretary again.

"You tell him I need him for five minutes, no more," I said. "And you tell him this: If he won't spare me five minutes right now, I'll send Arnold Mayer around to see him."

The secretary returned in about two minutes. "He'll see you now," she said. I asked Nelson to write a letter on behalf of my client, after having showed him the relative bids and the key material about the comparative products. My client retained his contract.

Then there were the odd jobs. Jimmy Hoffa, through my old colleague Sol Lippman (who had also left the Retail Clerks), hired me to find out if the White House, in granting Hoffa a pardon, had made a deal with the new Teamsters' leadership to include a provision keeping Hoffa from holding union office. Hoffa suspected that Frank Fitzsimmons, his successor, had promised to support President Nixon in return for a Hoffa pardon—but a pardon which assured that Fitzsimmons could retain power in the union.

My investigation was inconclusive, but I reported there was no doubt in my mind that White House aide Charles Colson had indeed engineered such a bargain, as much for his own gain as for Nixon's and Fitzsimmons'. When Colson left the White House (before Watergate descended on him, ending in a prison term and a conversion to Christianity) he joined a law firm in Washington, bringing to it representation of the Teamsters for $100,000 a year.

But with all the heavy contracts coming in—many of them referred to me by Republicans in Congress (the Democrats didn't seem to have many connections with private industry)—I often found that I could make my calls and contacts for my clients in little more than half a day. I started hitting the hangouts to see old friends. Some would join me for a quick drink and then hustle back to work. But while they each had one drink with *me*, I had at least one with each of the half-dozen people I might run into. I was putting on pounds, and I was afraid I was becoming an alcoholic.

So I started going home in the afternoons, instead. I'd flip on the television and watch "As the World Turns," "The Edge of Night" and an occasional afternoon movie. But I found myself hitting the liquor cabinet as well. While I watched the daily travails of characters in the soap operas, I was slugging down at least a pint of scotch.

173

Janice, meanwhile, had gone to work in the office of Speaker of the House Carl Albert. By the time she got home, I was in my cups, too tired to go out, and our social and personal life started dwindling to nothing.

For the first time in my life, I was making real money. And instead of enjoying it, I was boozing it away—along with ignoring my wife and family. I was risking my health and my happiness at the very time I should have been enjoying the new security.

Perhaps I was too immature to handle a sudden spurt of income. Perhaps I was wrong never to have developed a hobby like woodworking. Whatever the reason, it couldn't go on. I was getting too much for doing too little. It should have been fun, but I missed the action of tramping the hallways of Congress. And I was becoming a lush.

Part of my problem, I suppose, was a sense of malaise that was developing in me and, I believe, in much of the rest of the American people with the onset of the Nixon administration. For the first time since Dwight Eisenhower had sent troops to Little Rock to enforce a court desegregation order, the national commitment to black equality seemed to be eroding. Enormous and largely peaceable demonstrations against the Vietnam War were ignored disdainfully by Nixon and his men. What had begun in Johnson's last years with campus riots and the horrible Democratic National Convention in Chicago in 1968 seemed now to be getting worse instead of better.

It was in Chicago that I started nursing a deep foreboding about what lay ahead. Not only had the convention been a political shambles from which Hubert Humphrey could not recover, but—on a personal level—my wife had been overcome by a gas grenade one night as we strolled near Grant Park. It was because of that incident—being personally touched by the rage that was building in the country—that I recommended to White House aide George Reedy that he keep Johnson away from the convention. The spectacle of an incumbent President of the United States being unable to attend the political convention of his own party was, to me, exceeded only by the resignation in disgrace by Richard Nixon six years later.

174

But during 1969, I began feeling for the first time that my life was somehow out of control. Until then, I had been a political mechanic, working to add bits and pieces to the governmental engine without ever really looking to see what the whole car looked like or caring in what direction it was going to run.

Now it seemed the car was moving in an erratic circle. Not only did I feel helpless to stop it, I felt forlorn at having somehow contributed to its faulty workmanship. The system didn't seem to be working.

I didn't delude myself that I could make any impact on changing things in the country. But I felt that I had at least to get back into a job in which I could talk to the men and women who could. There were, for example, people like Senator Vance Hartke of Indiana whom I wanted to be in a position to help. Hartke was not deeply loved by the press, perhaps because of his intense personality, perhaps because of an old charge (never substantiated) regarding methods of raising campaign funds. Publicity about him had thus tended to overlook his considerable ability. But Hartke was a man who, among other things, openly stood up to Lyndon Johnson in opposition to continuing the reckless war in Southeast Asia. For his trouble, he was called "obstreperous" by the White House—and was placed in serious danger of losing his next election in 1970 to a candidate more in tune with the Administration's hawkish war policies.

Spending one half the day working on mergers or on procuring government contracts, and the other half swilling scotch, was not likely to help the Hartkes be vindicated at the polls. (He was defeated in 1976, but at least I was there to help elect him in 1970.)

So when I heard that the National Cable Television Association was hunting for a chief lobbyist, I lunged at it with Fred Israel's blessing.

NCTA is a complex organization. Its members included big-city cable systems who were frequently at odds with their country cousins over policy. Its leadership lacked cohesiveness and, at times, would present different faces to members of Congress on the very same issue.

Because the organization needed clout to minimize government regulation without, at the same time, dwarfing its chances to become competitive with network television or the motion picture industry, it was looking closely and painstakingly at all the applicants for the lobbying job.

My credentials were good and my brief stint in private industry and a dozen years with the labor movement didn't hurt.

But during my interview, I noticed that one member of the hiring committee, Bruce Lovett, kept slipping out of the room. He would return in a few minutes and nod knowingly to the others. It was some months later that Bruce, who became a close friend, told me what he had been up to.

When I recounted some of my work for President Johnson, Lovett left the room and put in a call to Walter Jenkins, once Johnson's closest assistant, who then was in the cable TV business himself in Texas. Lovett wanted confirmation that I had, in fact, done the chores for Johnson that I had claimed I had.

Later, I mentioned that I had run the campaigns for Hale Boggs of Louisiana to become the Democratic leader in the House of Representatives and, simultaneously, led Hugh Scott's campaign to replace Everett Dirksen as the Republican leader in the Senate.

My interviewers obviously were keenly interested in that piece of news and Lovett left the room to make some more telephone calls.

To be sure, my role in those successful efforts had gained for me—and, indirectly, for my clients—the enormously important opportunity to get appointments to see people at the highest levels of congressional policy-making in both houses and in both political parties. And they were campaigns that had to be pushed in differing manners. Boggs was opposed by, among others, Morris Udall, a brilliantly effective liberal congressman from Arizona. But Boggs was an old friend and, though further to the right than Udall, a man who was closer to the middle of the political spectrum in his party and therefore, in my opinion, then better able to develop party unity. Scott, meanwhile, was opposed by Roman Hruska of Nebraska and Howard Baker of

Tennessee. Of the three, Scott was considered by far the most friendly to labor and social causes.

So on the one hand, I was pushing Boggs because of his moderation and, on the other, helping Scott because of his relative liberalism. So to the Republicans in the Senate, my pitch was to avoid naming a "Neanderthal" as leader (which was an unfair but effective characterization of Scott's opponents), and to the Democrats in the House it was to steer clear of naming a "knee-jerk liberal." In both instances, to be fair to myself, I was working for men closest to the middle road—and I argued that such men would gain the greatest possible working relations with their respective parties and the greatest possible respect and credibility among the people.

One of the most effective methods I used was to establish—by word of mouth—that both Scott and Boggs were the odds-on favorites for their respective leadership jobs. A couple of carefully planted news items, identifying some key members who were quietly working for my candidates, strengthened that notion. Then I would call on the members and tell them, in effect, they had better get on the bandwagon. If they did, they could count on patronage assistance—good committee assignments for themselves and support for local projects that would help get them votes in their next campaigns. If they didn't, I suggested facetiously, good government might dictate that others, not them, would get the plums dispensed by the leaders.

Sometimes, the plums can be delivered subtly. I knew one congressman desperately interested in adding a dam in his district to the already committee-approved public works bill. To do that, he would have to offer an amendment when the bill was called up for a vote. He had already cleared his intention with the committee chairman, and the chairman had decided to go along with it.

But when the congressman decided to take a trip back to his home district, the leadership coincidentally decided to call the public works bill up for a vote. What happens in a case like that is the leader of your party will keep track of individual members' pet projects—and he'll either delay a vote or get a message

177

through to the traveling congressman to speed to Washington, or both. But this congressman had frequently opposed the leadership. So there was no phone call—and, subsequently, no amendment offered and no dam for his district. Whether it contributed to it or not, the congressman was defeated his next time out for office.

At any rate, I checked out and the NCTA hired me. For the next five years, I worked the halls of Congress in a new role. Strom Thurmond greeted me warmly and said, "Well, Chuck, now that you're not with those labor barons anymore, you and I can sit down and talk."

What we were to talk about for much of my career there was the move in Congress to adopt a new copyright law. Our concern was the growing demand that cable TV pay copyright holders for the programs it siphoned from the airwaves and presented to its viewers. The argument was that cable got these programs for free and should not. Our argument was that networks, in selling air time to advertisers, included cable TV viewers in their figures and so collected extra money because of us.

In this argument, the motion picture industry was against us. In another fight—to push for pay cable and access to up-to-date motion pictures—the motion picture industry was for us.

Much of my membership was adamantly opposed to paying any copyright fees. I adamantly opposed much of my membership. I argued that Congress was bent on establishing some form of copyright requirement covering us. If we simply opposed any payment, we would be hit by a payment schedule we either wouldn't or couldn't live with.

I proved to be much more persuasive among congressmen than among my own bosses. A committee proposal in the Senate finally emerged in 1974. It hit us between the eyes. It called for us to pay, on a sliding scale, between 1 and 5 per cent of our income from a particular show as copyright costs. And, at the end of eighteen months, a three-member congressionally appointed panel would re-examine the rates and adjust them if necessary.

In a high-cost, high-risk business like cable TV, that proposal would put a lot of our members out of business. Cable investors depended on big bank loans and few banks would be willing to lend large sums if they knew that in eighteen months, a tribunal in Washington might raise the copyright payments and thus reduce profits—and ability to repay loans.

At that juncture, my board of directors swung behind me and urged me to get the best deal I could. I first tried to get rid of the tribunal idea. But Hugh Scott reminded me that when the idea first emerged, I didn't object to it. "You're right," I conceded. "I made a mistake." Scott assured me it was too late to scratch the tribunal idea. My best bet, he advised, was to prolong the enacted rate schedule to assure banks and other lenders that a profit picture presented to them would not change in a short time.

I agreed. But my first job was to reduce the enacted payment scale. I sought guidance from Quentin Burdick of North Dakota.

"Some of my friends," he said laconically, "are for abortion. But others are against it."

"So where do you stand?" I asked.

"With my friends." He smiled.

I took the hint and bombarded the members by having their local cable TV owners implore them to reduce the rates. By mid-1975, we succeeded in getting the committee to halve the original proposal and to set the sliding scale from 0.5 per cent to 2.5 per cent.

Next, I went back to Thurmond and gave him my pitch on the need to keep a tribunal from re-setting the rates too quickly to be acceptable to the banks. I proposed the rates remain locked into law for ten years. He agreed with me. But he said I'd need a Democrat to join him in the effort or it would be viewed as a strictly conservative position. I decided to try James Abourezk of South Dakota, the lowest-ranking member on the Judiciary Committee, which was studying the bill. Newer members often are keen to sponsor bills so as to help establish a legislative track record. Besides, Abourezk was from a state in which cable TV played an important role in the daily lives of many of his constituents.

Abourezk bought the idea and, with Thurmond, pushed

through the amendment in committee to extend the review of rates from the original eighteen months to ten years.

Our worries weren't over. Senator John Tunney of California, representing the movie interests, tried to amend the bill when it reached the floor in early 1976 to make the first review of rates in five years instead of ten. It was George Washington's birthday and a number of senators had either not returned from a holiday weekend or were out campaigning as candidates running for President. We had the votes to defeat the Tunney amendment. That wasn't the problem. Unless a quorum of fifty-one senators is present to defeat a measure, it is permissible to bring the exact proposal to the floor again for another try. If we were to cut down Tunney's attempt to reduce the review period from ten to five years—and to keep him from gaining more time to persuade other senators to join him—we had to beat him then.

It is impossible for members of Congress to keep track of the thousands of bills on which they must act each year. Unless a bill is before a committee on which they serve, or unless it directly affects them or their constituencies politically, they take advice on how to vote from a limited number of people: their legislative assistants, the secretary of their party (who tells them what the party leadership advises), or from lobbyists they know and trust. In this case, however, the job was simple. I didn't care how anyone not yet accounted for might vote, as long as we got a quorum. We had the votes; we just had to make it stick.

I gathered up as many of my staff as possible and had them roam the corridors near the Senate floor looking for any stray members they could find so they could urge them to vote on the bill. We telephoned the offices to make sure every available body answered the vote. We got the number of senators to fifty when I spotted Gale McGee of Wyoming strolling just outside the Capitol.

"Senator," I pleaded, "we need you to vote on a bill of ours that's up for a vote."

"Sure, Chuck," he said. "How do I vote?"

"Senator, to tell you the truth, it doesn't matter to me. I need a quorum on the floor or they can bring it up again. We've already got enough to beat it."

En route to the floor, I outlined the proposal to him and he shrugged and said he'd be glad to vote for our side. I thanked him and he walked on the floor. We had the quorum.

Tunney tried two days later to bring up another amendment, this time lowering the review time from ten to eight years. By then, however, he had lost whatever momentum he had and his amendment was overwhelmingly defeated.

At about the time we won the copyright battle, I decided to leave the cable TV association. Again, as had happened at the Retail Clerks, there had been a change in leadership and the new president wanted his own team running things. But the association signed a contract with me to continue lobbying for them as a consultant. Similarly, I decided to develop other clients and, back in private business again, I'm starting to earn a considerable amount of money. This time, I'm five years older and, I think, better able to manage affluence than I was before. Besides, this time I'm sticking to what I know and love best—the Congress. Janice, meanwhile, left Speaker Albert's employ and joined a management consulting business. Both of us now walk the halls of Congress and even have time to have lunch together now and then.

It has often occurred to me that, while Congress debates a slew of new proposals to regulate lobbyists more stringently and determine more accurately how much time they spend for which of their clients and how much they are receiving for their efforts, it is overlooking one idea to make lobbying more effective for more people.

I think there ought to be a public lobbyist, a sort of ombudsman, a person appointed by the President and approved by Congress to serve a single ten-year term.

Bureaucracy has grown so big that neither the individual citizen nor the small company can effectively voice a complaint in Washington. A person or company with a few shekels to spend can get the services of a good lobbyist. But if you don't have the money, you simply can't get a fair hearing—just as you can't hire an Edward Bennett Williams to defend you in a criminal case unless you've got John Connally's money.

For instance, there's a small Ohio company I know that held a contract with a government agency. The agency decided to terminate the contract and award it to another, bigger company on the ground the Ohio firm's product was inferior. That company spent thousands of dollars in successfully challenging the contract cancellation. It was able to prove—though at substantial cost—that it's product was superior and that the other company had applied pressure to get the contract switched.

If we had a public lobbyist, he could sift through complaints from the people about unfair treatment from government. Some of this sort of thing—such as people not getting approval for an increase in their social security payments they think they're entitled to—is handled by congressmen. But they are perennially overworked and understaffed and they usually give preference to cases referred to them by local political allies. It's not that they don't want to help all their constituents with their problems with government red tape. It's just that they don't have the time.

Also, the General Accounting Office frequently issues reports critical of the operation of some executive branch agency or department. A congressman will make a speech about it and the press will publish the critique. But nine out of ten times, there is no substantial change because Congress is so overloaded with legislation it can't always conduct cogent hearings leading to a meaningful change. But many of the problems in the executive agencies don't require new laws or full-dress hearings. What they need are changes in regulations, the way they administer a program, the way they respond to an individual problem. A public lobbyist can pick up the ball from the General Accounting Office. He can effect a change within an agency or put it on his agenda to persuade the Congress to deal with the problem. The public lobbyist's recommendations regarding priorities on outside problems can have great effect on members—both on what they think is important to the people and on what they also think will get them some publicity and prestige back home.

For the time being, lobbyists will continue to be an essential part of making the Congress more responsive to private voices. To be sure, the voices that can afford representation will be heard above the others. But at least someone, acting through a

lobby—whether it's the oil lobby or the environmental lobby—
will, in fact, be able to communicate with Congress.

Without communication, most congressmen can only sense—
usually from a highly colored and parochial Washington view-
point—what the people need and want and have a right to ask
for. And faulty communication leads only to confusion.

Recently, when a national publication printed a report of my
role in the incident at Fort Bragg in 1968 where President Johnson thought he was talking to troops bound immediately for
Vietnam, I received a call from my father.

"That's a terrible thing you did," my father chastised.

"What was so terrible, Pop?" I asked, honestly puzzled.

"To dope a President, that's what. It says you 'confirmed that
the President was doped.'"

"That's *duped,* Papa, not doped. I confirmed the President had
been duped."

"Oh," he said. Then he added: "Well it's still not nice to dupe
a President. But it's better than doping him."

It isn't always easy to have good, clear communication among
people.

But that's what lobbying is all about—establishing communication between a segment of the population and those who
make the laws affecting it. You hear about the payoffs and, of
course, there have been some and, probably, there always will be
some. But the reason you hear about them is that they are the
exception, the rare exception, and not the rule. The rule is simply
someone or some group exercising its First Amendment right to
free assembly and free speech. As long as people, including
congressmen, know who the lobbyists are and whom they represent, lobbying has been and will continue to be an indispensable
adjunct to government.

In 1965, not long after Hubert Humphrey had been inaugurated as Vice-President, he made a speech at the twenty-fifth
convention of the Retail Clerks. In his remarks, he said:

"By the way, I was met at the door by my friend Chuck Lipsen. Chuck is about the best—I won't say 'lobbyist' because that
isn't what he is—but adviser and counselor to the Congress of
the United States. He does a great job."

That was nice to hear, especially from the Vice-President of the United States. But Hubert was wrong. I *am* a lobbyist.

I like what I do. There may be better occupations. But there are worse things. After all, I could have been a guy who goes around doping up Presidents.